MILLER

DEATH OF
A SALESMAN

NOTES

Revised by W. JOHN CAMPBELL, Ph.D.

Bound to stay open

Publisher's Note

Otabind (Ota-bind). This book has been bound using the patented Otabind process. You can open this book at any page, gently run your finger down the spine, and the pages will lie flat.

ABOUT COLES NOTES

COLES NOTES have been an indispensible aid to students on five continents since 1948.

COLES NOTES are available for a wide range of individual literary works. Clear, concise explanations and insights are provided along with interesting interpretations and evaluations.

Proper use of COLES NOTES will allow the student to pay greater attention to lectures and spend less time taking notes. This will result in a broader understanding of the work being studied and will free the student for increased participation in discussions.

COLES NOTES are an invaluable aid for review and exam preparation as well as an invitation to explore different interpretive paths.

COLES NOTES are written by experts in their fields. It should be noted that any literary judgement expressed herein is just that — the judgement of one school of thought. Interpretations that diverge from, or totally disagree with any criticism may be equally valid.

COLES NOTES are designed to supplement the text and are not intended as a substitute for reading the text itself. Use of the NOTES will serve not only to clarify the work being studied, but should enhance the reader's enjoyment of the topic.

"Death of a Salesman" by Arthur Miller
Copyright © 1949, by Arthur Miller, published by
Martin Secker & Warburg Ltd.

ISBN 0-7740-3023-2

© COPYRIGHT 1996 AND PUBLISHED BY
COLES PUBLISHING COMPANY
TORONTO—CANADA
PRINTED IN CANADA

Manufactured by Webcom Limited
Cover finish: Webcom's Exclusive **Duracoat**

CONTENTS

Arthur Miller: Life and Works

Arthur Miller was born in the Harlem section of Manhattan on October 17, 1915, the second son of a well-to-do clothing manufacturer whose eldest son followed him into the business. Arthur's interests, however, were football, hockey and, as he says, ". . . just fooling around." In fact, he was 17 before he read anything more serious than the Rover Boy books.

The Millers moved to Brooklyn while Arthur was still a young boy. He graduated from high school there in 1932 with a poor scholastic record, which prevented him from being accepted at the University of Michigan. He went to work in an auto parts warehouse instead, but soon became convinced that he really wanted to continue his studies at college. Miller was finally admitted to the University of Michigan in 1934, after waging an intensive campaign to get the admissions department to reverse its original verdict.

At the university, Miller began to write plays almost at once. In his sophomore and junior years, he gained a certain amount of recognition by winning the Avery Hopwood Award for the best student play. He failed to win the prize in his senior year, but he subsequently submitted the drama to the Theatre Guild whose National Award was given to him in 1938, the year of his graduation. He shared the Theatre Guild award with a southern aspirant one year his senior: Tennessee Williams.

Immediately after leaving the university, Miller joined the W.P.A.-sponsored Federal Theatre Project, then in its last years. While working with this group, he wrote a tragedy about the conquest of Mexico, which has never been published or performed. Miller remained with the Project until it ended. He then returned to New York where he earned his living for a few years by writing radio scripts, which he found an uncongenial occupation because, as he later observed, in radio drama every emotion must have a label. It helped to pay the rent, however, and made it possible for him to marry a college classmate, Mary Agnes Slattery. They had two children before the marriage ended in divorce.

In 1941, Miller was rejected by the armed forces because of a high-school football injury. He kept busy during the war years by writing scripts for army training films, working in the Brooklyn Navy Yard and visiting army camps where he gathered material for his first book, *Situation Normal*, published in 1944. It was during this time, too, that he did research for *The Story of G. I. Joe*, a movie about the well-known correspondent, Ernie Pyle. In 1945, Miller published his second book, *Focus*, the subject of which was anti-Semitism. Critics regarded it as "eloquent" but "too pat."

Since then, Miller has devoted himself almost exclusively to the theater. His first produced play was *The Man Who Had All the Luck*, written in 1944 and presented on Broadway the following year. It closed a week later. This failure was succeeded by a triumph—*All My Sons*—in 1947. This study of a dishonest wartime airplane-parts manufacturer established Miller's reputation. It won the three top awards in the New York theater: The Drama Critics' Circle Award, the Antoinette Perry Award and the Donaldson Award. A year later, *Death of a Salesman* was produced on Broadway. It won all the awards that he had previously earned, plus a Pulitzer Prize.

During the McCarthy era of the 1950's, Miller, whose politics represented the liberal intellectual outlook, was questioned by the House Un-American Activities Committee. He was indicted for contempt of Congress after refusing to answer questions about the activities of his acquaintances. One result of this legal altercation was *The Crucible*, a historical drama based on the Salem witchcraft trials with an implied analogy to the activity of the McCarthy group. The terror inspired even in innocent people, in both cases, the "handing over of conscience" to an outside authority, seemed to Miller a parallel too striking to go unremarked. When it came to Broadway in 1953, *The Crucible* met a mixed public and critical reaction, inevitably colored by the political temper of its time. It has been revived several times in America and has also found a warm reception from European audiences.

Miller's next plays, *A View from the Bridge* and *A Memory of Two Mondays*, were produced as a double bill in 1955. *After the Fall*, which marked his return to the theater after an eight-year silence, opened at the Lincoln Center Repertory Theatre in 1963. This thinly disguised autobiographical work received generally favorable critical reviews, although some observers felt that Miller was too frank with details of his second marriage.

During Miller's second marriage, to Marilyn **Monroe**, his only literary output was a motion picture scenario, *The Misfits*,

2

which he wrote for his wife in 1959. This movie was described by many critics as original and penetrating. Miller and Marilyn Monroe were subsequently divorced, and he then married a German photographer, Ingeborg Morath.

As a man of independent thought, Miller is profoundly and angrily concerned with what he perceives as the immediate issues of our society: the irresponsible pressures that are brought to bear upon free men, the self-seeking that blinds whole segments of our civilization to justice, the evasions and dishonesties into which cowardly men slip daily. To these convictions, he is able to add immense theatrical gifts. He knows how to make a point simple and obvious, how to give it bite in the illustration and how to make language ring out from the stage. He has not only the professional crusader's zeal for humanity, but the imaginative writer's feel for it.

"Mood plays" dismay Miller. "The pretense," he says, "is that nobody wrote them—they were just there." And he has no patience with what he sees as the present schism between philosophy and politics; his ultimate purpose is to weld them together as the Greeks and Elizabethans did. He has pointed out that Shakespeare and Sophocles had one thing in common: they both tried ". . . to draw a whole world into one man, to bring a national experience to bear on an individual subject."

Miller's plea is that we re-examine the premises by which we live. Each new work is meant to hasten the day when the present equation, man versus society, will give place to the ideal equation, man equals society. He sees the theater as a place where people must be made to think, as well as to be entertained. Though Miller's deep involvement with social issues is evident throughout his work, he is still basically a playwright and as such finds his greatest satisfaction. He has called his work, ". . . the only normal trade for a sensible man." A friend once observed that "For Arthur, an ivory tower is an uninhabitable slum " And, by Miller's own admission, he is driven to write by a sleepless social conscience.

Introduction to *Death of a Salesman*

Death of a Salesman opened on February 10, 1949, at the Morosco Theatre in New York. It was immediately acclaimed as that rare perfect blend of script, setting, staging and acting that is the true alchemy of the theater. Each element of stagecraft and drama seemed in perfect balance, and the result was a new substance, the stuff of classics, wherein the whole is greater than the sum of its parts. All the good adjectives were polished off and set in type to describe it; *The New Yorker* summed it up as a mixture of "compassion, imagination, and hard technical competence" not often found in our theater. The few dissenting voices came chiefly from the far right and the far left: on the one hand, it was said to be a "time bomb expertly placed under the edifice of Americanism;" on the other, it was termed "decadent." Nevertheless, *Death of a Salesman* was the high point of a good season, as its award-winning capacities indicated.

The reader of plays must always bear in mind the difference between the task of the playwright and that of the novelist. The novelist may visualize his audience as an individual with book in hand, but a playwright writes to a theater audience—a group mind—and he is necessarily dependent on all the other ingredients that constitute the theater as well as his own creative writing. Actors, producers, stagehands, musicians, scenery, make-up, costumes—all these and more compose the total final effect. Literature always asks that the reader meet the author halfway. With few exceptions, however, the play reader, as opposed to the playgoer, needs an extra measure of imagination and empathy to evaluate the work before him.

The commonplace manner of speech employed by Willy Loman, for example, has been termed dull by some, but as voiced by actor Lee J. Cobb, that dialogue came alive, and made a *person* of Willy. And persons, if seen whole, are always interesting. Again, the free movement of the play in time and space could be a source of confusion and must be followed with careful concentration in the reading. But played against a flexible set with effective music and lighting as guides and mood-makers, these methods seemed right and inevitable. In a word, they worked.

Try to bear this in mind as you read. Try to visualize the

action on the stage. For *Death of a Salesman* is a new approach to the problem of presenting time (and its passage and meaning) to a theater audience assembled for a brief two or three hours actual elapsed time. Many devices have been used to deal with the problem of the movement of time—from the classical Greek chorus giving us the word, to minutely realistic aging of the characters by means of make-up changes. So accustomed are we to most of these devices that we scarcely note their presence. At first glance, this play seems to be making use of the now familiar flashback technique. Closer study shows a significant difference, however. It is a new form, an effort to create a kind of constant NOW on the stage rather than a sequence of events. As the author puts it, *Death of a Salesman* "explodes the watch and the calendar."

Mr. Miller indicates that his first germ of thought for the play was a kind of vision of a man's head opening up so that we could see what went on inside. Even his first title for the play was *The Inside of His Head*. From this original idea, through to the final working script, Miller was absorbed by the concept that a man *is* his own past, that past and present exist together at all times in the man. He speaks of hoping to present Willy Loman's story as if it were one chord within which all the themes and melodies are contained, already made known. He wanted the audience to react, not with "What happens next and why?", but with "Oh God, of course."

This kind of procedure was in direct contrast with *All My Sons*, his previous success and a far more traditional play. The methods of bringing conflict to climax, through carefully timed relief of carefully prepared suspense, were methods Miller had studied and used. His success with the technical departure employed in *Death of a Salesman* was at least partly due to his command of the more usual techniques. From this grows his instinctive knowledge of the right time and the right reason to break away from established procedure.

But, of course, the play is more than an exercise in technique, for technique is only the means to an end. What were the author's intention and purpose? *Death of a Salesman* has been probed and analyzed and dissected from many standpoints: economic, psychological, metaphysical and literary. Miller's self-stated goal was to show a little man battling to make his mark in the world while maintaining his dignity intact. To show this picture as life, it is presented not ordered and structured, but in a myriad of disparate details which become related only as we make them part of ourselves and our experience.

The play was written over the comparatively short period of six weeks, and produced with only minor changes. It nearly had a different name: Miller's colleagues were sure that the gloom of the title would hang heavily over the box office, but his artistic judgment was allowed to prevail and to justify itself.

Death of a Salesman swept the award field for the year, winning the Drama Critics' Circle award, the Antoinette Perry, Theatre Club and Front Page awards, as well as the much coveted Pulitzer Prize. Road companies took it on tour. European productions in translation played to full houses. The printed edition was a Book-of-the-Month Club selection and set a sales record for plays in book form. The movie rights were snapped up and for some months it was the most popular title going in secondary rights for college and amateur productions. It was an altogether heady triumph, even for an author accustomed to the rarefied air of award-presentation ceremonies, and it was a triumph Miller has not been able to repeat, whatever the partial success or the true merit of his later work.

Arthur Miller's position in the literary history of the theater is not wholly definable as yet. This much we can say: on the basis of his three major plays, *All My Sons, Death of a Salesman* and *The Crucible,* he stands firmly in the line of dramatists dealing in social criticism, most of whom look to Ibsen as their founding father and George Bernard Shaw as their major prophet.

Miller represents a more subtle, more mature approach to this field than some of its early American practitioners, who tended to use the stage as a soapbox. For, although some critics find his work doctrinaire, on the whole he has followed Ibsen in another respect which helps him to avoid mere propaganda. Miller brings a basic realism to his stage, a true-to-life sense of dialogue and characterization so that his people are many-faceted personalities rather than mere symbols, and his action is telling a story rather than merely reading a lecture or the riot act.

We are accustomed to classifying plays according to labels from classical antiquity: tragedy, comedy, with melodrama and farce as later offshoots. Is *Death of a Salesman* a tragedy? Does the superficial symptom of the unhappy ending entitle it to assume the tragic mask? Is Willy Loman a figure sufficiently large to be a tragic hero? These questions are probably the most argued critical problems about the play. And if it is not tragedy in the true sense, what is it? Think of this as you read; it is a point to develop later on.

Such questions constitute a major reason for a drama student to read this particular play. The best literature excites thought; it does not wrap up and deliver answers in a neat package. Other questions will demand your thoughtful consideration. Does Mr. Miller put the blame for Willy Loman on society, or does he put it on Willy? Where does individual responsibility leave off and corporate responsibility take up the burden, or vice versa? To what extent is Biff the product of his father's influence? Has Linda done her husband a true kindness in playing along with his follies all these years? Try to formulate some working answers as you read.

Characters in the Play

Willy Loman: The central character in the play, Willy has been employed for 36 years by the Wagner firm as a traveling salesman. Now, at the age of 63, he has been removed from salary and placed on straight commission, a sign that he is no longer as valuable to the company as he once was.

Linda Loman: Willy's wife. She is devoted to the welfare of her husband and has made many sacrifices in order to sustain him. She tries to support and encourage Willy, yet despite her efforts he grows increasingly depressed.

Biff Loman: Willy's 34 year old son, the elder of the two children. As a high school student, he was a star football player and showed great promise for the future, yet he has spent the past 14 years attempting to find meaning in life.

Happy Loman: Willy's 32 year old son, the younger of the two brothers. Happy is independent, lives in his own apartment and works for a department store. He feels rejected by his father, who always preferred Biff.

Charley: A next-door neighbor and lifetime friend of the Lomans. When Willy is put on commission, Charley lends him money each month. He is more down-to-earth than Willy and more successful.

Bernard: Charley's son. As a child, he was Biff's friend and has gone on to become a successful attorney.

Jenny: Charley's secretary.

Ben: Willy's dead brother. As a young man he left home and became very wealthy. He is the man Willy was never able to be, and he appears in Willy's daydreams as the only man Willy ever met "who knew the answers."

Howard Wagner: Willy's boss at the Wagner company and the son of the original owners. It is he who puts Willy on straight commission.

Miss Francis: The woman with whom Willy has an affair in Boston.

Letta & Miss Forsythe: Two young women picked up by Happy in a restaurant.

Stanley: A young waiter at Frank's Chop House who talks with Happy.

Plot Summary

As the play opens, Willy Loman, who has been a traveling salesman for 36 years, returns home after having just departed for a sales trip to New England. He tells his wife, Linda, that he can no longer go on the road because he cannot keep his mind on driving his car.

This coincides with a visit from his elder son, Biff, who is staying at the Brooklyn home after being away for many years. Willy reminisces about Biff's potential, 14 years earlier, when he was playing high school football and being offered athletic scholarships by numerous university teams. Later, we learn that Biff did not go to university because he failed high school mathematics. His failure led him to go to Boston, where Willy was at the time, in an effort to get Willy to influence the teacher to change his marks. Unfortunately, Biff discovered Willy having an affair with a woman in the Boston hotel room. This precipitated Biff's drifting through life.

When we meet Biff, he is discussing future job prospects with his younger brother, Happy. Biff considers going to see Bill Oliver, a man for whom he had worked many years earlier, and asking him for a loan to get started in a sporting goods enterprise. Biff and Happy tell Willy of this plan and he gets very excited with the idea. He emphasizes that Biff is well-liked by Oliver and we begin to see Willy's fixation with the idea that one only needs personal attractiveness to be successful in the business world.

In fact, Willy decides that he, too, will go to see his boss the following day and ask that he be given a New York posting rather than a traveling job. The first day ends with the bright hope that both Willy and Biff will succeed the following day in achieving their goals. Willy, Biff and Happy plan to meet for dinner the following evening, after they have been to their respective meetings.

Willy is not successful in his meeting with Howard Wagner, his current boss and son of the deceased owner. Wagner tells him that he cannot find a place for Willy either in New York or on the road. He tells Willy that he is fired because he is doing the firm harm. Willy is crestfallen and can only go to see his old friend and neighbor, Charley. Charley loans Willy enough money to pay his life insurance premium and we learn that Willy has been borrowing $50 a week from Charley for a long time. Charley offers Willy a job, but Willy cannot bring himself to accept it. While at Charley's office, Willy meets Bernard, Charley's son, who has become a very successful lawyer. Bernard wonders why Biff lost his initiative 14 years ago. This angers Willy and causes him to reminisce about the past.

Biff and Happy meet in the restaurant for dinner. Biff explains that he has come to some important realizations about himself following his planned meeting with Bill Oliver. Apparently, Oliver kept him waiting all day and then could not remember who Biff was. Biff was so upset that he stole Oliver's fountain pen. This leads him to reconsider all of his previous jobs, which he lost because he could not keep himself from stealing.

Willy arrives at the restaurant and tells Biff that he has been fired. When Biff begins to tell Willy that he stole Oliver's pen and has been a failure all his life, Willy refuses to listen to the truth and gets up. At this point, Willy's daydream takes him back to his moment of infidelity in Boston and he is shaken by it. Biff leaves the restaurant and asks Happy to make sure Willy is all right, but Happy rejects Willy and departs with two girls he has picked up.

When Biff arrives home later that evening, Linda is furious with him for having deserted his father. Willy is in the backyard planting seeds and holding an imaginary conversation with his dead brother, Ben. Ben had been a very successful man. During this conversation, Willy lights upon the idea of committing suicide. This idea is reinforced after Biff and Willy have an argument and Biff collapses sobbing on Willy. Willy is convinced that Biff loves him and so he proceeds with his plan, believing that the insurance money of $20,000 will set Biff up for life.

Willy commits suicide and only his immediate family and Charley attend his funeral. Nevertheless, Biff gains an insight into himself, though Happy swears he will follow in the "noble" footsteps of Willy.

Summaries and Commentaries
by Act and Scene*

ACT I • SCENE 1

Summary

The play opens in Willy Loman's house. Willy, a salesman for the Wagner company, enters the kitchen exhausted. Earlier that morning he had left on a business trip, but soon realized that he was unable to keep his mind on the driving. Consequently, he turned around and drove back home.

His wife Linda enters and expresses concern over Willy's early return. It is clear that Willy is tired and that, despite a recent vacation in Florida, he lacks energy and enthusiasm for life. Linda believes he is mentally fatigued: "Your mind is over-active," she tells him.

Though they live in New York, Willy services the New England region. It is, no doubt, an escapism for him which allows him to keep home and job separate: he can leave his work problems behind in New England, and the same is true of his domestic troubles when he sets out on a sales trip.

Willy feels he is not appreciated by his boss, Howard Wagner, son of the founder of the company. Willy decides to talk to Howard Wagner.

Biff and Happy, Willy's two sons, are home for the first time in many years. When Biff first arrived, Willy criticized him for the life he has been leading. Biff has not yet "found himself" and Willy fears that his son is losing valuable time: "How can he find himself on a farm? Is that a life? A farmhand?" He ascribes Biff's present situation to laziness and wonders why he has come home. Linda claims that Biff is "very lost," and in a speech which contradicts what he has just said, Willy answers that Biff's problems have nothing to do with laziness. Whenever Willy is angered by his son, he lashes out in criticism. Other people, however, are not permitted this freedom and Willy is quick to defend Biff in the face of criticism by others. Willy decides to have a talk with Biff in the morning and help him get a job in sales.

Life in the city has begun to prey on Willy. He longs for the time when his neighborhood was less congested, less polluted: "The way they boxed us in here. Bricks and windows, windows

12

---

* NOTE: Arthur Miller made no scene delineations in the original play. Here changes of theme and the entrances and exits of characters are used to divide each Act into scenes.

and bricks." He recalls with nostalgia the garden and perfumed air of yesterday.

Commentary

Arthur Miller wastes no time in presenting his major character, the salesman Willy Loman, and the man's principal conflict: the hopeless pursuit of an elusive success. Like most salesmen, Willy is a dreamer. He has aspirations to financial and personal grandeur, but his inability to achieve his goals has reduced him to a state of desperate, drawn fatigue. His emotions are in upheaval and it depresses him to see his son Biff, a man of immense "personal attractiveness," lost in the process of finding himself.

Arthur Miller states in an essay from his *Collected Plays* that "Willy Loman does not merely suggest or hint that he is at the end of his strength and of his justifications; he is hardly on the stage for five minutes when he says so; he does not gradually imply a deadly conflict with his son [Biff], . . . he is avowedly grappling with that conflict at the outset." Biff has the attractiveness which Willy believes necessary to be a success in life, particularly as a salesman. Willy sees himself in Biff and wishes to relive his life through Biff's success. But Biff has not yet amounted to anything, and this is doubly discouraging for Willy, for not only is his son a disappointment after having shown such early promise, he is also depriving Willy of fulfillment through his offspring.

The relationship between the two men is central to the drama. The interplay between them serves to further the action and intensify the conflict at work within Willy's mind. Miller is not leading to a conflict which will become exposed in the last act, rather, he announces the conflict at the beginning of the play and uses the rest of the time to clarify the problem. To be sure, there is a climax at the play's end, but the nature of this climax can be seen as early as this first scene — indeed, as early as the play's title. All leads to Willy Loman's death, and what is shown here as a moral and spiritual deterioration eventually winds its way into the actual physical death of the protagonist.

Willy's anxieties are deep. His mind is full of thoughts which surge back and forth from past to present, leaving him in a state of confusion and irritation. When writing the play, Miller decided that the path to Willy's destruction lay in making him recall his past: "If I could make him remember enough, he would kill himself, and the structure of the play was determined by what was needed to draw up his memories like a mass of tangled roots without end or beginning." This process, which serves as the structural basis of the entire play, is evident in this first scene. Willy tells Linda that he couldn't keep the car from going off onto the side of the road and that he had opened the windshield and "just let the warm air bathe over me." As he tells this to Linda, he adds: "I have such thoughts, I have such strange thoughts." It turns out that Willy's mind has lapsed and he believed he was driving his old 1928 Chevy, a relic from the last happy period in Willy's life. It was then that his son Biff was a football star and that Willy felt his life was successful.

The motif of nature is significant in Scene 1 for two reasons. Willy recalls his old neighborhood as having had lilac, daffodils, wisteria and peonies. It was a time when his vision of life was no doubt fresher and his enthusiasm higher. The set-backs of his middle years had not yet plagued him and his ambition and optimism about the future was at the forefront of his existence. Now things have changed. He is no longer a young man and his career as a salesman has become less productive. His dreams for success now seem impossible to achieve. Nature, then, represents something pleasurable and untainted in Willy's imagination. He sees it as an unrestraining, free, and hopeful terrain on which to act out the great accomplishments of life. On the other hand, it is also the site of escapism for him, something which distracts him from the cold reality of his present turmoil. Driving up to New England is tantamount to escaping the viciousness of New York. He tells Linda: "It's so beautiful up there, the trees are so thick, and the sun is warm." Willy's reality becomes less and less based in the visible, tangible world. Instead, he becomes lost in the tone and character of past actions. This is what Miller meant when he referred to Willy's destruction via thoughts. Once Willy abandons himself to the workings of his mind, there is no escape for him. He is doomed to self-destruction and can be saved by no one. He is intuitively aware of his crisis. When he explains to Linda about his inability to keep the car on the road, she replies that he may need new glasses. But Willy knows better: "No, it's me, it's me." The rest of the play is devoted to portraying the deterioration of this salesman and, ultimately, his death.

ACT I • SCENE 2

Summary

While Willy and Linda are talking, Biff and Happy raise themselves up in their beds and listen to their parents. Willy tells her that she is his foundation and support, and Linda tries to soothe his anxieties. It is very important to Willy that his son Biff be happy in life and he tries to let Biff do what he wants: "If he wants to go back to Texas, let him go." He believes in his son's ability to make something of himself.

Linda suggests that they take a drive on Sunday and that they can open the windshield. When Willy replies that "the windshields don't open on the new cars," it is clear that he was dreaming earlier that day when he told her he had opened the car's windshield. He realizes what has happened and finds it peculiar: "I was thinking of the Chevvy. Nineteen twenty-eight . . . when I had that red Chevvy — That funny? I coulda sworn I was driving that Chevvy today." Again Linda attempts to minimize the importance of Willy's lapse. For Willy the car represents a period of happiness, a time when life was easier for him.

Overhearing their parents' conversation, Biff and Happy exchange comments on their father. Biff believes he will lose his license if he keeps up with such lapses of attention, and Happy adds that Willy doesn't seem to keep his mind on what he is doing: "I drove into the city with him last week. He stops at a green light and then it turns red and he goes."

Happy radiates sexuality and seems content on the surface while Biff, though well built, is less self-assured and has had fewer successes. Biff is the favored older son however, and Happy looks up to his brother, the one who taught him everything he knows about sexuality and women.

The two brothers think back with nostalgia on their childhood. Biff wonders why Willy now mocks him all the time, but Happy believes the man just wants Biff to be successful. Yet Happy knows that Willy has a problem: "Something's happening to him. He talks to himself. It got so embarrassing I sent him to Florida." He says that Willy spends most of these mumbling sessions talking to Biff.

Biff reminisces about the time he has spent since high school trying to make a life for himself. The idea of working at a daily job, struggling for a salary, is repugnant to him but he knows that this is how one builds a future. He realizes a pattern has emerged in his life. Although happy with each job through the rest of the year, each spring he suddenly feels that life is passing him by, that he is accomplishing nothing: "I suddenly get the feeling, my God, I'm not gettin' anywhere!" This is why Biff has returned home. But when he gets there, he doesn't know what to do with himself.

Happy, who is successful in the sense that he has a permanent job and draws a regular salary, explains to Biff that none of his achievements has brought him real happiness: "It's what I always wanted. My own apartment, a car, and plenty of women. And still, goddammit, I'm lonely." When Biff proposes that the two of them buy a cattle farm out West, Happy clings to his present situation, claiming that he wants to prove to his mediocre superiors that he can do a better job than the current merchandise manager.

Biff mentions that a former employer named Bill Oliver might be in a position to lend him several thousand dollars. With this money, he could buy a ranch. They overhear Willy talking to himself, carrying on an imaginary conversation with Biff. It is the re-creation of a scene which occurred years earlier when the boys were still children.

Commentary

The importance of this scene is to show the bond of fraternity between the two brothers, Biff and Happy. While their lives have grown apart in the years since high school, they are nonetheless capable of relating on a reasonably intelligent level about the problems confronting human beings trapped in a lifestyle of resentment and frustration. While Happy appears successful in one sense, he is actually bored by his job and unmotivated to develop himself for the future. What interests him primarily is the idea of eventual revenge, of demonstrating to his employers that he can do well as manager of the merchandising department. Money and material success are not his goals since they, by themselves, serve no purpose. They do not bring happiness, nor do they eliminate the daily frustrations of the job.

Biff knows that he is in trouble with his life and wants desperately to do something about it. But he does not know how. He lacks definition and organization, and lives his life on an essentially physical level. He would like to find a woman with whom he could have a permanent relationship, but so far this has not happened. Like his brother, he knows that something is missing in his life, that he lacks fulfillment and that he must work toward something if he wants happiness in the future. It's the idea of drudgery as a worker which repels him; the endless performing of unpleasant and uninteresting work is an obstacle which has paralyzed him.

Both Biff and Happy show themselves to have been influenced by their father. They are intrigued by the notion of living on a ranch in touch with nature, and they have discovered the torture of living life in a world of illusions. To what extent they have been molded by Willy Loman will be made more obvious in the following scenes.

ACT I • SCENE 3

Summary

As Biff and Happy finish talking, Willy is seen downstairs in the kitchen. He spends most of the scene talking to Biff, even though he is alone in the room. He warns his young son not to talk seriously to girls, to take his schooling first and then worry about dating. Willy has regressed to a time when his sons were younger. His monologue reveals a preoccupation with a life which was simpler than the present one, a life where the concerns included polishing the car, cutting down a tree branch and so on.

Commentary

The purpose of this scene is to demonstrate the extent to which Willy's conflicts have confused his thinking. The pain of reality forces him to regress to earlier, happier times, particularly those involving the young Biff and Happy. There is nothing unusual about the act of remembering the past and savoring its delights. The problem here, however, is that for Willy the past is taking the place of the present.

Willy's fundamental love for his children makes for a touching dramatic moment and provides further insight into the depth of his frustration at their failures.

ACT I • SCENE 4

Summary

This scene takes place entirely in Willy's imagination. Young Biff and Young Happy appear, and we realize that Willy is reliving former moments of pleasure from the period of his children's youth. The boys have just finished washing and waxing Willy's car and he congratulates them on the fine job. As a gift to them, he has purchased a punching bag. Happy seems eager to have Willy's attention and approval, but Willy favors Biff. The latter has removed a football from the locker room so that he can practice with it, and when Happy reproaches him for doing so, Willy comes to Biff's defense: "He's gotta practice with a regulation ball, doesn't he?" Though Willy does not approve of the theft, he is adamant about defending his favorite son, even at the expense of the other one's feelings.

The boys tell Willy they were lonesome for him while he was on his latest sales trip. Willy confides in them his dream of having his own business one day; that way, he'll never have to leave them again. Happy asks if the business will be like Uncle Charley's. He is their next-door neighbor and not a blood relation. Willy retorts that his business will be much larger than Charley's.

Willy tells them that his recent trip took him to Providence, where he met the Mayor, then on to Boston. It will be revealed later that this is where he had the affair with Miss Francis. All the important people in New England know him, he claims, and this impresses his young admirers. Willy promises to take the boys on a trip with him in the summer. Then they discuss the upcoming Saturday football game, and Biff promises to score a touchdown just for his father.

Commentary

While the first few scenes of the play show Willy's conflict in its present, aggravated state, this scene gives us a feeling for the period which preceded his eventual downfall. Willy was already talking to his boys in exaggerated, self-inflating tones, emphasizing his importance in the New England region. The boys do not yet know any better and so they worship this man whom they judge to be a true hero. He is their father and they love him. Anything he says is recorded by their minds as Truth,

18

and this sets them up for later disappointment when they realize what he actually represents.

Already Willy tells them he can be more successful than Charley. This is an example of Willy's sentiment of total invincibility. He believes that he can surpass the accomplishments of anyone, yet he fails to build the necessary foundation for arriving at that phenomenal success. Charley, in the minds of Biff and Happy, is a success, and it excites them to think that their father can own a company even greater than Uncle Charley's. Of course none of this comes true. It is one more promise of grand achievements which can take place only in Willy's mind.

Miller depicts Willy in this scene as a man desperate to win the affection of his sons. The gradual stripping away of their illusions creates the dramatic pathos which follows. We suspect at this stage that his trip to Boston is not the success he claims it to be. Only later will we see that Willy's unhappiness and lack of fulfillment has already gotten the better of him. He has become involved with another woman and is in violation of the All-American family and dream which he wishes to represent.

These happy times of 1928 will be the last pleasant memories for Willy. From that period onward, everything will fall apart for him.

ACT I • SCENE 5

Summary

Charley's son, Bernard, enters, dressed in knickers. This scene is a continuation of the last one, taking place entirely in Willy's mind. Bernard is younger than Biff, earnest, loyal and a worried boy. He asks Biff why he isn't studying with him, and Willy comes back at him with: "Hey, looka Bernard. What're you lookin' so anemic about, Bernard?" A tone of threat is introduced when Bernard says that Mr. Birnbaum, the teacher, said that Biff would fail math if he didn't start studying. This would prevent him from graduating, and is the first time we see Biff in a less than flattering light. The high school star may well go astray and wander from the path of success. It is perhaps the realization of this which prompts Willy to say: "You better study with him, Biff. Go ahead now." Bernard leaves, and Willy asks the boys whether the child is well liked. They reply: "He's liked, but he's not well liked," which is a direct quote of what Willy had said to them earlier about Bernard's father, Uncle Charley.

Willy tells his sons that they will be much more successful in the business world than Bernard because they are physically well built and attractive, "built like Adonises." Willy speaks about the success of men who have personal attractiveness, and though it has a ring of truth to it, one realizes that it does not apply to Willy Loman himself. Rather, it refers to the ideal man which Willy would like to be. He does not have the kind of personal attractiveness which he commends, but he knows it would help him if he had it. Happy ends the scene by reminding Willy that he, Happy, is losing weight.

Commentary

Willy's statements about personal attractiveness make this a symbolically important scene. Willy sees himself as more of a success than Charley, yet the opposite is true. The same parallel exists between Bernard and Biff. Biff is the football star who can do no wrong while Bernard is mocked for being anemic and something of a study wart. In point of fact, Bernard turns out to be much more successful than Biff and spends time as an adult playing tennis on his friends' tennis courts. Willy represents the dream of "anything is possible," but he fails to incorporate into this dream a sense of organization, dedication, hard work and sacrifice for the sake of the long-term effect. Biff and Happy have their minds filled with Willy's ideas, and it comes as no surprise that the children enter adulthood with distorted ideas about success. Willy preaches superficiality, surface appearance and magnetism instead of integrity, absolute truth and hard work. He prefers to make life seem glamorous in his attempts to impress his sons, but what he does not realize is that he is damaging their ability to assume responsibility as grown men. Biff's later belief in himself as the most important human being around will cause him considerable trouble when he is unable to accept orders from employers. All of this stems from Willy's lessons to them.

ACT I • SCENE 6

Summary

This scene continues in the past as Linda enters with a basket of washing. Biff takes it from her and calls downstairs to his friends, instructing them to sweep out the furnace room. Clearly they worship him, just as Biff does Willy. The two sons go outside to hang up the laundry.

Willy lies openly to Linda about his recent sales: "I'm tellin' you, I was sellin' thousands and thousands, but I had to come home." This whole business of seeking an escape in his imagination is one which will prove to be fatal to Willy. As a man in his 60's, he will realize that his past was not the bed of roses he sometimes thinks it was. When the memories become bitter and traumatic, he will be unable to find pleasure in them and will be forced back to the duress of reality. For the moment, however, he continues to indulge in a fantasy about his self-worth as a younger man and claims to have made lots of money while in Boston. He is forced to adjust his figures when Linda asks about his real commission. She needs money to pay the bills and he realizes that he can no longer lie about his profit: "The trouble was that three of the stores were half-closed for inventory in Boston. Otherwise I woulda broke records." Linda tells him that they need to pay for a refrigerator fan belt, a vacuum cleaner, a washing machine repair job and so on. When she mentions that they owe money for the Chevrolet's carburetor, he screams in anger that "they ought to prohibit the manufacture of that car!" But only a moment earlier, he had extolled the virtues of the same car with: "Chevrolet, Linda, is the greatest car ever built." His statements reflect momentary emotion rather than committed belief.

When Willy realizes that he has not made enough money to pay the bills, he sinks into sadness about his abilities as a salesman. Initially he states that he'll go up to Hartford, where he is very well liked, but then he changes his tune with: "You know, the trouble is, Linda, people don't seem to take to me." This is the ultimate tragedy of Willy's existence. His moments of lucidity are poignant and dramatic; he senses that people laugh at him, but doesn't know why. He sees himself briefly as an ineffective salesman, one who must spend ten or twelve hours a day making sales while other men get by on much less. In his own private way, he admires Charley, whom other people respect. He thinks he is fat, but Linda compliments him and tries to soothe his fears.

Commentary

The truth about Willy comes out in this scene: he is too

21

talkative on the job, makes too many jokes, has been criticized for being over-weight and knows that people neither like him nor respect him. It takes a tremendous amount of courage to be able to make those comments about himself, especially to the woman he loves, but we see him here as a pathetic, lonely, desperate man — one who knows that he is not at all the person whom he has portrayed to his sons. It is a good example of illusion versus reality. The boys believe in the illusion because it is what Willy tells them, but in the recesses of his mind, Willy understands that he is a failure. His emotions are in turmoil, as witnessed in his contradictory statements about the Chevrolet, and his mood shifts are characteristic of someone on a collision course with trouble. Linda makes every attempt to praise him for his good looks, sales ability and sense of humor, but it is in vain. Willy knows the truth and cannot escape the nightmare of his inadequacies.

ACT I • SCENE 7

Summary

As Willy and Linda are having their conversation, a new dimension is added to his re-created past: the Woman (Miss Francis) is seen dressing, off to the left of the stage. Her laughter is heard as a taunting, disturbing sound in the background as Willy tells Linda how much he loves her and how he wishes she could be near him when he's out on the road. The laughter becomes louder as the Woman arranges her hat, standing in front of a mirror. Willy underlines the fact that he gets very lonely on his sales trips and feels a need to be close to Linda: "I get the feeling that I'll never sell anything again, that I won't make a living for you, or a business, a business for the boys." He talks through the Woman's subsiding laughter but stops when Miss Francis tells him that it was she who chose Willy, not the other way around. This flatters his male ego and he begins talking with her. She claims to appreciate his sense of humor, but we also learn that Willy has given her new stockings from his sales kit.

Willy takes her in his arms, but she says she must leave. It is late and her sisters will be scandalized but she promises to return in two weeks when he's back in the Boston area. The scene ends on a jarring note as the Woman's laughter mixes with Linda's.

Commentary

We now have an insight into the extra-marital affair which Willy has had with Miss Francis in Boston. He has become involved with her because of his loneliness, but there is also the idea that he is flattered by her interest in him. Since Willy does not see himself as a desirable person, it is exciting for him to think that a woman would choose him over all the other men in her life. Despite her motives, Willy sees her as a reinforcing agent to his masculinity, and ultimately to his ability to do things at which men are supposed to excell — such as selling. The scene arouses sympathy for Linda, who remains at home while Willy is on the road. She has no notion of his infidelity and maintains her stance as a loving, supportive wife. This makes Willy's unfaithfulness even worse since he has two sons and a wife at home who believe he is a hero. Miller uses this infidelity to underline the eventual tragedy which befalls Willy. The infidelity adds to the explosive atmosphere as Willy realizes he has neither the ability to sell his wares nor his own personality. It serves as one more detonator to the delayed explosion which lies ahead.

ACT I • SCENE 8

Summary

When the Woman leaves, Willy's thoughts return to the conversation he was having with Linda in the kitchen. She compliments him on his handsomeness, not realizing that she is contributing to his false identity, his illusion of success. Willy, exiting from the area where he and Miss Francis were together, hastens to reassure Linda that he'll make it all up to her. There is no indication that she knows what he is talking about. She says to him: "There's nothing to make up, dear. You're doing fine." He is angry that she is mending stockings, perhaps because he recalls having given new ones to Miss Francis. He orders Linda to throw them out.

Bernard enters, looking for Biff. They need to study for the Regents exam and Biff hasn't been studying. Willy suggests that Bernard provide Biff with the answers, but Bernard replies that this is impossible on such an exam. This is another indication of Willy's willingness to overlook honesty in an effort to make everything possible for his son.

Willy falls into a rage about Biff in a sudden mood swing. Everything negative about the boy converges at the same time and it is more than Willy can bear: Biff has stolen the football, drives without a license, refuses to study for the exams, is too rough with the girls and so on. Willy decides to whip his son and we hear laughter from the Woman in the background. Willy suddenly abandons his anger toward Biff when others begin to criticize him too. He asks whether Linda would have her son "be a worm like Bernard." The atmosphere becomes haunting, disturbing and desperate. Bernard, Linda and Miss Francis are, for Willy, instigators of unrest. They drive him further into his inner nightmare as they force him to consider certain truths about Biff and himself.

Commentary

This is the most uncomfortable scene thus far in the play. It is a clear demonstration of Willy's emotional turmoil and shows the workings of a troubled, confused mind. He is ill-equipped to deal with all the negative forces. He orders Miss Francis to shut up and resorts to screaming at both Linda and Bernard. Here we see Willy beginning to lose control, and it marks the first serious step toward his suicide. His memories of the past are no longer utopic or joyous; they are filled with sadness and regret, and threaten to destroy the imaginary peace which Willy believes existed in days gone by. When he reaches the point where his imagination and memories are no longer pleasant, he will have nowhere to go to escape the present and so he chooses death. His present situation in life is intolerable, and this will be worsened by an agonizing past which refuses to leave him alone. Neither the illusion nor the reality will be possible for Willy.

ACT I • SCENE 9

Summary

As Willy sits alone talking to himself, we return to the present. Happy discovers him in the kitchen and Willy becomes aware of his presence. He explains to his son that he nearly hit a child in Yonkers that morning and that this shocked him into returning home.

Willy regrets not having gone to Alaska with his brother Ben when he had the opportunity several years earlier. The man was an enormous success and could have helped Willy. He had begged Willy to go, but it was in vain. Happy says he will support Willy in his retirement and that he should not worry about anything. But Willy finds this hard to believe: "You'll retire me for life on seventy goddam dollars a week? And your women and your car and your apartment, and you'll retire me for life!"

Charley walks in from next-door. He is a large man, slow of speech and has pity for Willy. He has seen the light on in Willy's kitchen and has come to make sure that everything is all right. Happy leaves the two men alone.

Charley takes out a deck of cards and they begin to play. Charley asks why Willy is home and the salesman explains that he had had car trouble. Charley mentions that he might go to California and offers Willy a job. Willy is offended, sensing that Charley knows something about his present situation. This causes him resentment, embarrassment and humiliation, and he yells at his friend.

Willy changes the subject to Biff. He cannot understand why his son wishes to go back to Texas, but Charley advises him to let things develop naturally, to forget about Biff. Willy is stricken by the thought of putting Biff out of his life: "Then what have I got to remember?" Memory is Willy's only source of pleasure.

Uncle Ben, Willy's brother, enters carrying a valise and an umbrella. He is, of course, dead and Charley cannot see or hear him. But he enters into Willy's thoughts and the two have a conversation. Charley tells Willy that his name is not Ben. Willy announces, as if he knew his own death were near, that he has gotten awfully tired in life. Willy snaps back to reality and realizes he has called Charley by his brother's name: "For a second there you reminded me of my brother Ben."

Ben tells about some properties he is looking at in Alaska. It is a re-creation of a conversation which the two brothers had at some point in the past. Willy confesses that Ben was "the only man I ever met who knew the answers." All this is a bit perplexing to Charley because Willy keeps slipping in and out of the past, conversing in part with Ben and in part with Charley. Willy tells Charley that Ben died a couple of weeks ago in Africa. Then everything becomes confusing for Willy, who cannot juggle the statements coming at him from both Ben and Charley. He loses the sequence of events and finds himself unable to focus on either Charley or Ben. In an attempt to dispel his confusion he insults Charley by insinuating that Charley has made an improper move in their card game. He cannot bear to think that his neighbor is in any way better than he. Charley departs.

Commentary

This scene is of value in situating Willy's growing confusion between the past and present. It underlines his regret over not having gone with his brother Ben to Alaska where he might have become a true success — Ben eventually became the owner of a diamond mine. It also shows his resentment toward Charley, who has made something of his life. Both Charley and Ben have been successful, but Willy prefers his brother's kind of success. Ben walked into the jungle of life at age 17 and came out rich at age 21, while Charley represents the more cautious, practical kind of businessman. Ben's sense of daring appeals greatly to Willy.

The idea that Happy might provide financial assistance to his father is one which Willy would love to entertain, but which he cannot accept openly because it would mean failure and a hopeless dependence on his off-spring. It is one more avenue which closes Willy off from life. He is an aging salesman who can no longer provide for his family and he has no means of producing money for the future. Moreover, the fact that his favorite son, Biff, wishes to return to Texas causes Willy sadness. He is unable to shut Biff out of his life since this would involve turning his back on his greatest source of potential happiness. But Biff's indecision about life leaves Willy confused.

ACT I • SCENE 10

Summary

Charley has left the room, and Willy remains alone with the spirit of his brother Ben. It is a memory being re-enacted rather than an actual confrontation with a ghost. Linda enters and asks Ben where he has been all these years — Willy has been waiting for him. Ben relates how he had originally set out for Alaska, but went in the wrong direction and ended up on the Gold Coast of Africa, where all the diamond mines are located. The young Happy and Biff rush into the room and are introduced to their Uncle Ben. He tells the boys that it only took him four years to become fabulously wealthy. Willy uses this as an example for his sons of how anything can be accomplished in life when one sets one's mind to it.

During the scene, Ben keeps looking at his watch. He is the stereotype businessman who thrives on deadlines and long working hours. Ben tells about their father, who made his own flutes and sold them across the country: "Great inventor, Father. With one gadget he made more in a week than a man like you could make in a lifetime." Willy boasts that this is the way he is raising his sons: "rugged, well liked, all-around." Ben dares Biff to punch him in the stomach and, after a rapid sparring match, Ben trips the boy to the floor and holds an umbrella to his eye, almost as a sign of what the powerful can do to the weak.

Ben makes a move to leave, after having warned Biff never to play fair with strangers. Linda bids him an icy farewell, but Willy feels a need to impress his brother before the latter escapes: "Boys! Go right over to where they're building the apartment house and get some sand. We're gonna rebuild the entire front stoop right now! Watch this, Ben!"

Charley enters and cautions that the police will catch them if they steal any more sand. Ben laughs at this, but Linda is upset. Willy gloats over the fact that his sons stole some lumber from the building project a week ago. Ben admires Biff's nerve, and Willy joins him in laughter.

Ben gets ready to leave as Willy confesses his uncertainty about himself. Their father left the family when Willy was very young and this had a tremendous impact on his sense of direction: "Can't you stay a few days? You're just what I need, Ben, because I — I have a fine position here, but I — well, Dad left when I was such a baby and I never had a chance to talk to him and I still feel — kind of temporary about myself." This is a major revelation into Willy's character.

Commentary

There are several important points to consider in this scene. The fact that Ben had originally set out for Alaska and arrived in Africa indicates the role of chance in life. There is no way to tell whether his luck would have brought him tremendous riches in Alaska, yet he became a wealthy man through sheer determination and hard work. He was lucky to have discovered himself in a locale which offered the chance to get ahead, yet he would have failed if he had not been shrewd enough to take advantage of his situation. Willy believes that his problems would have been solved if he had accompanied his brother on the journey. Perhaps he would have benefitted from the proximity to his brother. On the other hand, Willy might have done equally poorly in Africa. The essential point is that Willy has not taken advantage of the myriad opportunities in the New England region and will never find the riches his brother did. Luck is not enough; hard work and ingenuity are just as important.

Ben is an example of success for the boys. But he is also Willy's idol. Ben is the man Willy would love to have been. His success is the fuel which excites Willy, but even Ben realizes that life is a jungle, that one cannot play fair in the game of competition. Willy has some fundamentally good qualities, such as love for his children, but is blinded by the dazzle of money and, as a result, cannot hope to imitate his brother. Willy wishes to impart to his boys that one can have everything one wants in life. Yet as Ben demonstrates, *wanting* to be rich is not enough; you have to work for it. There is no trace of this ethic in Willy's teachings to his sons. Glitter and glamor eliminate all consideration of system and organization in Willy Loman's approach. Perhaps Miller chose the name Loman since it resembles Low-Man: Willy will always be the low man on the totem pole of life.

The idea of time plays an important role in this scene. Ben looks at his watch and makes comments about his need to leave. This act is somewhat symbolic of the motif of time passing by in Willy's life: the clock is running out on Willy and, unlike his brother, he has nowhere exciting to go. His destiny is the fabric of dreams and impractical thinking.

Miller introduces the notion of Willy's father as a salesman — and a successful one, according to Ben. This is tied in with the fact that Willy did not know his father very well. His choice of a sales career can be seen, therefore, as an attempt to imitate his successful father, to re-create something of his father's presence, and to discover meaning in a world which is basically unwelcoming to a confused young man. Willy sets himself up as a model for his two sons, but at the same time he is in competition with the image of a successful father. The success was continued by Ben, but not by Willy, and it is understandable why Biff and Happy have not developed into highly successful people. Their role model programmed them for a lifestyle which was not possible within the guidelines of reality.

It is significant to consider Willy's need to impress his brother. This is directly related to his need for attention, love and support. It is an example of a childhood need which has not been satisfied and which continues long into adulthood. Willy is insecure as a human being as well as in his career as a salesman. The speech in which he reveals to Ben that he feels "kind of temporary" about himself is one of the most poignant, moving speeches in the play. It is, in fact, the clearest example of the insecurity which undermines Willy's ability to cope with life as a responsible, realistic adult. It is an enlightening moment in the tragedy of Willy's existence.

ACT I • SCENE 11

Summary

The time is now in the present. Linda enters the kitchen where Willy is seated; and urges him to come to bed, but he is restless. He begins to take a walk in his slippers when Biff comes into the kitchen in his pajamas. Biff is alarmed at Willy's behavior, but Linda hushes him up, fearing that Willy will hear them. She claims that Willy's odd conduct will pass by the morning. Happy enters and announces that he has never heard his father talk so loudly. Linda replies that he should come to the house more often because then he would hear it.

Linda explains to the boys that they need to show more responsibility toward their father — visits, letters and so on. Willy is at his worst when the boys come home. She says to Biff: "When you write you're coming, he's all smiles and talks about the future and — he's just wonderful. And then the closer you seem to come, the more shaky he gets, and then, by the time you get here, he's arguing, and he seems angry at you."

Linda asks why Biff is so hateful toward Willy, and he replies that he is trying to change. He doesn't know what he wants from life, but Linda is impatient with this attitude. She feels that Biff must appreciate Willy or he cannot possibly have any feeling for her: "You can't just come to see me, because I love him. He's the dearest man in the world to me, and I won't have anyone making him feel unwanted and low and blue." Biff is infuriated with his mother. Willy never paid Linda any respect and "wiped the floor" with her, but Happy interrupts and argues with his brother. Linda shows, for the first time, a genuine appreciation for who Willy Loman is as a human being. She describes him in terms which indicate an accurate assessment of his strengths and shortcomings: "I don't say he's a great man. Willy Loman never made a lot of money. His name was never in the paper. He's not the finest character that ever lived. But he's a human being, and a terrible thing is happening to him. . . The man is exhausted." She tells her sons that, after 36 years with the same company, Willy has been switched from salary to commission. Moreover, he has been borrowing $50 a week from Charley and has pretended to Linda that this was his pay. In her anger, Linda lashes out at her sons, calling Happy "a philandering bum" and telling Biff that he no longer loves his father as he once did. Biff replies that it was Willy who threw him out of the house. Biff believes his father is a fake, but won't explain why. In a moment of panic, Linda blurts out: "He's dying, Biff." The boys are shocked and she tells them that Willy has been trying to kill himself: after a car accident, the insurance man informed her that Willy had planned everything. She weeps while confessing that Willy's life is in Biff's hands. The boys argue about responsibility in the business world and Biff concludes with: "We don't belong in this nuthouse of a city! We should be mixing cement on some open plain."

Commentary

The drama is advanced one step further in this scene as we discover that Willy has taken steps to end his life. He has rigged several car accidents and has placed a rubber hose on the spout of a gas pipe in the basement.

The strength of Linda's character is presented in full force as we see the caring of a woman desperate about the welfare of the man she loves. Linda is shown as an intelligent, sensitive person who is willing to accept sacrifice if it can benefit another human being. She is justified in her anger toward her sons since they have, despite themselves, contributed to Willy's downfall. But the situation is complicated since they are not entirely to blame for their actions. Their adult lives are an outgrowth, in part, of their childhood training, and when they realized that

Willy's values were idealistic, they opted for lifestyles which excluded him. Happy lives closer to home than Biff, but we should recall what Willy told Happy in response to his offer of financial support. Willy knows that Happy is involved with his car, apartment and girlfriends, and this would suggest that there is little place for a father. As for Biff, Willy can neither live with him nor without him. When Biff is in Texas, Willy is worried and melancholy, and when Biff returns home, Willy becomes argumentative and irritable.

Most important in this scene, is the message contained in Linda's various speeches. She has a conscience and is not willing to reject a human being because of his age, problems or temperament. She is an excellent medium through which Miller can communicate many of his social ideas to his audiences. Miller has often been likened to Ibsen, whose problem plays present aspects of human nature which the dramatist expounded upon through his characters. Such is the case here.

ACT I • SCENE 12

Summary

Willy joins the conversation and announces that no one in the business world thinks he is crazy. This is in response to Biff's earlier statement — "They've laughed at Dad for years." Willy tells Biff to go back out West and be a carpenter, to enjoy himself; the salesman is hurt and speaks in short, choppy sentences. A verbal brawl sets in between Willy and Biff, but it ends quickly when Willy discovers that Biff is going to see Bill Oliver in the morning. Biff implies that he might open a business selling sports goods, with Oliver's financial backing, and Willy launches into a full-fledged show of support for his son's talents. Happy has an idea; they could create a sports line called the Loman Line and could form sports teams which would play each other: "It's a million dollars' worth of publicity. Two brothers, see? The Loman Brothers." Willy is entranced by the idea, and when Linda adds her enthusiasm, he tells her not to interrupt. An argument ensues when Biff comes to Linda's defense and Willy shouts him down for "takin' over this house." Willy exits suddenly, in a guilt-ridden frame of mind; he looks beaten and dejected. Happy suggests they go upstairs to cheer Willy up. As the two brothers leave the stage, Happy

31

can be heard congratulating Biff on his new burst of self-confidence.

Commentary

The danger of Willy Loman's philosophy of life is exposed in all its detail throughout this scene. Happy's idea about the formation of the Loman Brothers company incites an exuberance and energy in Willy which has not been evident in some time. In a sudden shift of moods, he becomes positive, excited and ready for the kill. What this means, however, is that he is prepared to take up the illusion of success which he has nurtured for years, but which, in the long run, is nothing but an illusion. This is summed up by Happy when he explains his idea to his brother: "And you wouldn't get fed up with it, Biff. It'd be the family again. There'd be the old honor, and comradeship, and if you wanted to go off for a swim or something' — well, you'd do it! Without some smart cooky gettin' up ahead of you!" These words summarize what Willy has aspired to in his lifetime: self-reliance, the ability to do what he wants whenever he chooses and the comfort of the family system as a functional unit.

But Willy has been prevented from achieving his dream because he has never understood the manner of building a successful business. He knows somehow that he has used ineffective tactics throughout his sales career and this is what prompts him to caution Biff about his behavior with Bill Oliver: "Don't wear sport jacket and slacks when you see Oliver. . . . A business suit, and talk as little as possible, and don't crack any jokes." He instructs Biff to do precisely the opposite of what he, Willy, has done all his life. But this practical advice is offset by a speech in which he throws all business sense out the window and re-assumes his role of Mr. Successful: "Remember, start big and you'll end big." This is Willy's most fundamental error. He has never realized the importance of building a business from scratch. He wants to start at the top, and this leads to his repeated failures in the business world.

The scene is an unsettling chain of conflicts, with moods shifting back and forth more rapidly than ever. Before a meaningful dialogue between two characters can gel, the mood has shifted again to an opposite emotion and the dialogue is cut off. But one thing is certain at the end of this scene, Willy will never be a success. And since it is highly unlikely that the idea of the Loman Brothers will meet with approval from a financial backer, it seems his sons won't be either.

ACT I • SCENE 13

Summary

Upstairs in the bedroom, Linda asks Willy if he can repair the leaky faucet. This throws Willy into a rage about how everything is falling apart. She wonders whether Oliver will remember Biff and Willy again remarks on his son's extraordinary potential. The boys enter and say good-night to Willy, but he cannot resist a few last words of advice. He tells Biff to lie about his past, to fabricate a story about having been in business out West instead of in farming. As Willy sinks back exhausted, Happy announces that he is going to get married; Linda replies to him: "Go to sleep, dear." Linda hums Willy to sleep. Biff goes downstairs and removes the rubber tubing from the gas outlet.

Commentary

This scene is useful for toning down the emotions aroused in the former scenes. Willy senses that everything is falling apart and he lies back in bed, exhausted. He begins to reminisce aloud about Biff's high school glory as a football star and this gives him some peace as he drifts asleep. This is Miller's way of reminding us that Willy's conflict is by no means resolved; but the playwright also realizes the importance of winding down the dramatic intensity as the Act comes to a close. This will enable him to build to a new intensity in Act Two.

Note the parallel structure of Willy talking to his boss Howard Wagner in the morning about being transferred to the New York region, and Biff talking with Bill Oliver about a business loan. This parallel structure allows us to see the attempts of both men to bring change into their lives. But we suspect already that neither will succeed.

ACT II • SCENE 1

Summary

The scene takes place in Willy's kitchen. It is the following morning and Linda has prepared breakfast for her husband.

When she comments that he looks well rested, he replies, ironically: "I slept like a dead one. First time in months." Biff has left to see Oliver, and Willy feels so good about things that he suggests buying some seeds for the garden. Linda claims that nothing will grow there anymore, and Willy expresses his desire for a house in the country where they can grown vegetables and have animals.

They discuss their finances and Linda reminds Willy to ask for an advance from Howard Wagner. It is disheartening to Willy that everything he owns tends to break down before it is paid off: "I'm always in a race with the junkyard!" They have one more mortgage payment, after which they will own the house. Linda tells him that he is to meet his sons for dinner at Frank's Chop House, where the three men can celebrate their business triumphs. Willy exits. He is on his way to speak with his boss about the job transfer.

The telephone rings and it is Biff. Linda announces with glee that the rubber tubing over the gas pipe has been removed and that Willy has done this himself, but Biff tells her that he took it away, not Willy. She reinforces the importance of what Biff is doing for his father: "Be loving to him. . . . You'll save his life."

Commentary

The Act begins on a prophetic note when Willy announces that he has "slept like a dead one." He means he has slept extremely well, yet the idea of his suicide is evident to the reader. He bears a sense of peace which is something like the calm before a storm. One knows already that Willy's moods swing rapidly, and that this peace can last only as long as there are no obstacles to confront.

In a symbolic vein, Willy mentions buying some seeds for the garden but Linda answers that nothing will grow in their yard: "Not enough sun gets back there. Nothing'll grow any more." She implies that at one point in their lives, growth was possible but that it has been killed off by deadening forces. In Willy's case growth is impossible because he has choked out reality with his exaggerated illusion. Ironically, the very reality which he has shunned for years (e.g. building a business from the basics, having a realistic picture of himself and his sons) is the agent which comes to claim his life in the end. Reality, which he has fled, comes to knock him down with all its force. It is no longer an opponent against which he can compete.

In Linda's telephone conversation with Biff, it is clear that she is both the eternal optimist and the down-to-earth realist. On the one hand, she hopes desperately that it was Willy who removed the rubber tubing from the gas pipe (i.e. optimism), but on the other hand she knows the importance of Biff's love to her husband (i.e. realism). What she fails to understand, however, is that the concept of "you'll save his life" is a major responsibility for Biff, who is in most ways an irresponsible man. We know that this responsibility is doomed from the start and that Biff will be unable to save his depressed father.

ACT II • SCENE 2

Summary
Willy meets with Howard Wagner at the office. Howard is intrigued with a new machine which has just been delivered — a tape recorder — and makes Willy listen to his children on tape. He is proud of them and they take precedence over anything Willy has to say.

Willy tells him that he would rather not travel any more: "I'm just a little tired." Howard has little sensitivity and replies that there is nothing available for Willy in the New York area. His wording is ironic: "There just is no spot here for you," as if he means in the entire company, not just in New York. Willy becomes desperate. Although he began the conversation by saying that he only requires $65 a week, he now lowers that figure to $50.

Everything that Willy has advised Biff not to do in a business situation (e.g. talk too much, show his nervousness), Willy does in this scene with Howard: "Just let me tell you a story, Howard —", Howard cuts him off with a cold, calculating answer, yet Willy plods on with his story of Dave Singleman, a salesman who lived to be 84 years old. Singleman was a role model for Willy. He made sales to twenty or thirty states by simply picking up the phone and calling people. Willy admired the respect with which he was treated and when he died, hundreds of salesmen came to his funeral. Then Willy lowers his salary demand to $40 a week.

Willy is infuriated because Howard tries to hurry him out of the office, claiming that there are other people he needs to see. Willy reminds him that in 1928 he averaged $170 a week in commissions, but Howard denies this. Howard has no interest in hearing stories about his father or about how Mr. Wagner, Sr., admired Willy. Howard tells Willy that he no longer wishes him to represent their company: "You need a good long rest. . . . Whenever you can this week, stop by and drop off the samples. You'll feel better, Willy."

Commentary

This is a complex scene from a psychological standpoint. The differences between Howard and Willy are enormous. Howard has achieved a level of career success which Willy lacks. He has a maid, a car radio, a tape recorder and a home atmosphere of relaxation where carefree children can play like normal, unpressured children. Willy's home is one of tension, strife and anxiety; he is overwhelmed with unpaid bills, has been a failure in his career, does not have the material possessions which Howard does and has children who are a disappointment to him. Howard has a future to look forward to, Willy has nothing. There is no rapport between the two men since Howard is unwilling to show any sensitivity. It is difficult to say what happened in the past between them: perhaps Willy has been a constant nuisance, an unproductive salesman, someone who has been more of a liability than an asset to the company. Because of this, it may have been necessary, for business reasons, to let go of Willy, even though it seems on one level that he is being thrown out the door like an inanimate object. Willy must, however, take responsibility for his own actions. It is not Wagner's fault that Willy has led himself into a dream world based on illusion. Howard does not seem like a man with tact or inborn sensitivity, especially in statements such as, "You didn't crack up again, did you?" But he is responsible for the well-being of his company and, unlike Willy, he takes his duties seriously. The tragedy, of course, is that one senses something productive about the younger Willy Loman. His early days as a salesman might have been much more successful than the present. Certainly the potential was there. But now Willy is a tired, older man and no longer has the energy to start anew. When Howard turns him down, Willy has nowhere to go. This sets us up for the encounter in the next scene between Willy and his dead brother, Ben.

ACT II • SCENE 3

Summary

As Howard exits from his office, Willy sits there stunned. Ben enters, carrying his valise and umbrella. Willy pleads with him for help and Ben says he needs someone to look after some timberland in Alaska. He recommends that Willy get out of the city. As usual, Ben is in a hurry. Linda enters, dressed in her work clothes, carrying a load of wash. She is part of Willy's daydream. She is not interested in the Alaska deal, claiming that Willy has a fine job in the city. She is not ambitious as Willy is and has no desire to conquer the world. Ben has no time for Linda's caution and begins to leave. The young Biff and Happy enter and Willy sings their praises. Willy attempts to explain to Ben how one becomes a success in the world, but Ben isn't taken in by him.

Commentary

This scene offers us little new information on the plot or character development. It is largely a review of what we have already seen. When Willy is tormented by reality, he reverts to his memories, fantasies and imagination. In this case, his discussion with Wagner became heated and, when Howard exited, Willy sat there alone, frightened and confused. It was a panic situation for him and, in order to cope, he sought refuge in his mind. But even there he finds little relief. He argues with his own brother and uses the example of Dave Singleman, a successful salesman, to convince Ben that a successful sales career can be made in the city.

When Ben offers Willy a job, Willy fails to act on his desire for improvement. Linda voices her opinion that Willy is doing extremely well in his present situation, no doubt an echo of what Willy has been telling her. His lies and distorted perceptions of his career success have gotten in the way of a promising venture with Ben, and this underlines even further the errors of Willy's judgement. He is trapped by his own fiction and does not wish to humiliate himself in front of his wife, who believes that he is a genuine success.

ACT II • SCENE 4

Summary

Ben has left and the young Bernard rushes in. He is excited

about going to Biff's football game at Ebbets Field, and Biff allows him to carry his shoulder pads to the clubhouse. Willy gives everyone a pennant to wave when Biff runs onto the field. Biff promises that when he takes off his helmet, it is a signal that the next touchdown is dedicated to Willy. Charley enters and Willy tells him, ironically, that there is no room for him in the car. Charley is confused as he knows nothing about the football game and had only come by in order to shoot some casino. Charley cannot believe that Willy has not heard the news: Ebbets Field just blew up! Willy tells him off for this joke and Charley laughs, wondering when Willy will ever grow up.

Commentary

Willy has become obsessed with Biff's football talents to the exclusion of everything else. He is unwilling to tolerate Charley's humor on a day when Biff is preparing himself to be a sports hero. Willy's values are arranged so that a football game becomes more important than the feelings of his friends, family or his business affairs. He is emotionally immature, and this is what distinguishes him from Charley, whom he resents and criticizes.

ACT II • SCENE 5

Summary

This scene takes place in the present. Willy has left Wagner's office and has gone to see Charley. His mood is sour because of the daydreaming about his next-door neighbor.

At Charley's office, Bernard, now mature, sits whistling to himself; a pair of tennis rackets and an overnight bag sit on the floor beside him. Bernard is on his way to Washington to try a legal case and will be staying with a friend who owns a tennis court.

Charley's secretary, Jenny, asks Bernard to attend to Willy Loman, who is alone in the hall and making a lot of noise about Biff's touchdown. When Jenny asks Willy how he is feeling, he replies: "Not much any more."

Bernard mentions that he has heard about Biff's arrival in town. Willy gloats over the "big things" that Biff is involved with, in particular the Bill Oliver deal. Willy fabricates lies in order to inflate Biff's importance. When asked whether he is still with the same firm, Willy dodges the question and compliments Bernard on his achievements. In a moment of intense emotion, Willy's voice breaks and he is barely able to speak. Quietly, he asks Bernard: "What — what's the secret? . . . . How — did you?" He wants to know the secret of being a success, and in the process shows himself to be a pathetic, beaten man. He confesses that nothing good has happened to Biff since Ebbets Field, and Bernard answers with: "He never trained himself for anything."

Bernard wants to know why Biff did not go to summer school when he failed math, an experience which crippled Biff for life. In resentment, Willy relates how Biff had come up to Boston to talk with his father when he should have been in summer school. Biff was gone for a month, and when he returned to New York, he took his sneakers and burned them. He and Bernard then had a fist fight because Bernard knew that Biff had given up. Bernard asks Willy what actually happened during Biff's stay in Boston. Willy becomes defensive and refuses to answer.

Commentary

Miller shifts the scene from Wagner's office to Charley's office without mentioning what he is doing. The transition is achieved by use of the football reminiscence. Willy begins daydreaming about the football game at Ebbets Field when he is still in Wagner's office. The same fantasy continues while he is en route to see Charley. This accounts for his behavior when he arrives at Charley's office and shows to what extent an isolated example of accomplishment (i.e. Biff's athletic prowess) has become the hallmark of Willy's pride. The passage of time is handled subtlely, as are the scene changes. The reader will notice that the action shifts from the past to the present, and while this happens, the scene shifts from the Wagner company to Charley's office.

Willy is on an emotional rollercoaster and is intimidated by the atmosphere of success in Charley's company. When the secretary asks him how he has been feeling, his reply is at the same time ironical and inappropriate: "Not much any more." It reflects muddled thinking and a shakey grasp on reality.

Bernard and Biff have reversed their earlier roles in life. The athletic Biff has become sedentary and drifting in his adult life while the clumsy Bernard developed an affinity for tennis. Biff's early successes faded into endless defeats while Bernard's hard work as a child paid off in his growing law career. He is on his way to defend a case in the Supreme Court and is entirely modest about it. Since he possesses self-confidence and a feeling of direction in life, he has no need to prove himself to others. The Supreme Court case is but one example of his responsibilities as an attorney.

Willy crumbles in Bernard's presence when he realizes that his facade of success no longer works. He tosses aside his lies about Biff's big business deals and pathetically asks Bernard for advice. Bernard rejects the role of advice-giver, but focuses on the more important question of Biff's high school failure. The encounter between Biff and Willy in Boston was centered around his affair with Miss Francis. In light of this, Willy's failure as a husband and father is linked to Biff's inability to cope with summer school. Once Biff learned the truth about his father, he was unable to finish high school and became disillusioned with life. The failure of the father is at the root of the failure of the son.

ACT II • SCENE 6

Summary

Charley enters this atmosphere of tension where Willy is yelling at Bernard for demanding some answers about Biff's trip to Boston. Charley announces that Bernard is on his way to the Supreme Court and Willy is astounded. The young man hadn't even mentioned why he was going to Washington. Bernard leaves.

Charley gives Willy $50 and explains that his accountant is waiting to see him. Willy needs $60 more to pay his insurance, so Charley sits him down for a chat. He has offered Willy a job which would pay him regularly and in which he would not have to go on the road, but Willy has turned him down. Charley wonders what is going on in Willy's head. He is insulted by Willy's attitude toward him and wants nothing to do with him. Willy argues hopelessly that he already has a job, knowing full well that he has been fired. Just as Charley had asked him nine years earlier before the Ebbets Field football game, he asks Willy: "When the hell are you going to grow up?" Willy is infuriated and calls him a "big ignoramus." He prepares to fight with his neighbor. Charley gives him the money for his insurance and tells him that it is not necessary to be well liked in order to be a success. Willy, near tears, thanks him and says Charley is his only friend.

Commentary

This is a traumatic scene for Willy, one where he is stripped of all honor and dignity. He is close to the end and must ask for a few extra dollars from his friend in order to pay his bills. His conflict with the idea of success is so great that he is unable to accept Charley's job offer even though he needs the money. His pride is gone, and all that remains is hatred: hatred for himself, hatred for being a failure and hatred at the idea of being humiliated before a friend. He is unable to throw off a lifetime's worth of values. If he were to adopt the system represented by Charley, it would be the same as admitting failure in his own life, and Willy cannot bear the agony of such a defeat. Whereas Willy always claimed to take a great interest in his sons, Charley did not do this. Willy's approach led to failure, but Charley is a success. This amazes Willy, especially now that Bernard is arguing a case before the Supreme Court, but Charley replies quite objectively: "My salvation is that I never took any interest in anything." Charley rejects Willy's emphasis on personal likeability, citing the despicable J.P. Morgan as an example of an unlikeable, but successful person.

This interaction with Charley places Willy at the lowest point in his descent from the illusion. Having turned down Charley's job offer, having been fired by Wagner, having been forced by Bernard to focus on the origin of Biff's failure and having lied to Linda about the state of his affairs, Willy now has nowhere to go. He is trapped by his own illusion and cornered without hope.

ACT II • SCENE 7

Summary

The scene shifts to Frank's Chop House where Stanley, the waiter, is talking with Happy. He is to have dinner here with Biff and Willy. While he's waiting, Happy flirts with a woman who claims to be a cover girl.

Biff enters in an agitated state. He waited six hours to see Mr. Oliver. At five o'clock, Oliver came out of his office and did not even recognize him. Biff feels numb from lack of self-confidence and tells Happy: "How the hell did I ever get the idea I was a salesman there? I even believed myself that I'd been a salesman for him! And then he gave me one look and — I realized what a ridiculous lie my whole life has been! We've been talking in a dream for fifteen years." Biff articulates what Willy has been fighting not to recognise.

Biff explains further that when Oliver left, he entered the man's office and stole his fountain pen. Then he ran down eleven flights of stairs: "I ran and ran and ran." Biff asks Happy how he should tell Willy what happened. Happy replies that Biff should tell Willy a lie and let him believe that Oliver will consider making them a loan.

Commentary

This scene gives us insight into the thoughts and feelings of Happy and Biff. Happy has chosen to celebrate the success of his brother and father before knowing any of the details of their respective dealings: he does not know that Willy has been fired, nor does he know that Mr. Oliver failed to remember Biff. Happy prolongs the illusion of success, as originated by Willy Loman, when he puts on false airs with Stanley the waiter and with Miss Forsythe, the cover girl. He places an order for an expensive meal and tells Miss Forsythe that Biff is a "great football player" with the New York Giants. The name of the football team which he selects at random is symbolically important. His brother has always been a sort of 'giant' to him and he finds it difficult throwing off this image of success. Like his father, Happy spends money on an event which turns out not to be a successful one. He is convinced that a big enterprise can be launched, but he pays no attention to the obstacles which are lined up against such a business.

Biff is desperate about his encounter with Mr. Oliver. His illusion is flattened by the man's refusal to see him and he realizes all too clearly that he has been living a dream. The pain of reality hits him head-on and leaves him feeling panicky. The facade of adulthood is stripped away, exposing a frightened, vulnerable child. This accounts for his infantile act of stealing the fountain pen. It is not an object of any worth, but the act is symbolically necessary so as to fulfill his desire for revenge on Oliver. It is an impulsive, irrational decision which leaves Biff all the more uncertain of his maturity. Happy notices this emotional strain and reminds him that he is "not showin' the old confidence." Biff's flight from Oliver's office is symbolically parallel to his flight from reality and from the problems of his life. When he understands what has happened, he is anxious for an answer. This is what prompts him to tell Happy: "You gotta help me."

ACT II • SCENE 8

Summary

Willy enters and they all order double scotches. He wants to know about Biff's conversation with Oliver and Biff tries nervously to explain. He attempts to remain factual instead of slipping into the usual 'everything's wonderful' routine. He reminds Willy that he was never a salesman for Oliver, rather, he was only a shipping clerk. Willy, in a burst of anger, announces that he was fired today: "I was fired and I'm looking for a little good news to tell your mother, because the woman has waited and the woman has suffered . . . . I haven't got a story left in my head, Biff. So don't give me a lecture about facts and aspects." Willy does not wish to hear the truth, he wants a glossy success story. Willy decides that Oliver recognized Biff and gave him a warm welcome, and Happy agrees. Willy asks him questions about the interview and makes it difficult for Biff to be honest.

Commentary

The dramatic technique in this scene is brilliant. Miller structures the dialogue so that the wires of communication are crossed when Biff, Happy and Willy attempt a conversation. Willy is determined to hear that Biff succeeded with Oliver, and Happy wishes for Biff to maintain this illusion for their father. Biff, however, is disgusted with dishonesty and tries to remain truthful throughout. So when Willy interrogates him about Oliver, Biff asks him about having been fired. When Willy forces an optimistic angle to the Biff/Oliver conversation, Biff re-routes the story back to the truth. Infuriated with Biff's approach, Willy finishes by shouting that Biff probably insulted

Oliver. All efforts at honesty are choked out by Willy's inability to listen. Biff had never worked for Oliver as a salesman, yet this is the version which Willy told whenever he related to anyone that his son was Oliver's employee. When Biff discovers that he has been living a lie, he desires a correction of facts and pursues the truth with his father. Willy is not interested in the truth. If a fact threatens his dream world, Willy will have no part of it.

ACT II • SCENE 9

Summary

This scene takes place on two levels: on the one hand, Biff, Willy and Happy are still in the restaurant and it is the present, on the other, Willy's mind wanders to the past and he introduces memories into the present conversation. This creates a sense of confusion and tension in the narration of what happened between Biff and Mr. Oliver.

Young Bernard is seen running into the Loman house, but the reader must remember that this is taking place only in Willy's mind. Happy urges Biff to tell Willy about the experience with Oliver, but Willy interrupts with scolding comments about Biff's failure in high school math: "If you hadn't flunked you'd've been set by now!" Biff begins to relate the Oliver episode, and Happy attempts to stop him. The lights on stage become dim, which parallels Willy's determination to shut his mind to the truth. The young Bernard announces to Linda that Biff has flunked math and that he won't graduate. Biff has already left for Boston to see his father. As Willy's thoughts return to the present, he becomes aware of the fact that Biff has stolen Oliver's pen. But just as quickly, Willy's mind recreates a painful scene from the past: the affair with Miss Francis. Biff is horrified to see what is happening to Willy and gets down on one knee before his father. For the first time in the play, Willy seriously rejects his favorite son: "You're no good, you're no good for anything." Biff tells him that he will make good and that Oliver has arranged to discuss a loan with his partner. But he also reminds his father that he stole some balls from Oliver years ago. This, coupled with the theft of the fountain pen, does not look very good. We hear the laughter of Miss Francis in the background. Willy believes that Biff is spiting him and, in desperation, he strikes his son. Miss Francis tells Willy that someone is at the door and at that moment Miss Forsythe (the cover girl) arrives back at their restaurant table with a friend, Letta. This juxtaposes the Woman in Boston (Miss Francis) with the cover girl with whom Happy was flirting. Willy is torn between his memories of the past (with Miss Francis asking him to answer the door) and the demands of the present (with Happy and Biff introducing him to the cover girl). Willy leaves for the bathroom. Biff yells at Happy for wanting to leave with the women instead of helping their father: "Don't you understand what I'm talking about? He's going to kill himself, don't you know that?" Happy disowns Willy when Miss Forsythe's friend asks him a question. Happy and the women run out of the restaurant, ready to "paint this town."

Commentary

Willy's thought processes have now begun their final descent. He is caught between the horrors of the present and the agony of his past. There is no longer a streak of happiness on which to depend and he resorts to physical violence with Biff.

Happy is completely without scruples as he abandons his father and leaves with the women. Having disowned Willy, he also disowns what his father represents, but at the same time launches forth on a binge of selfish pleasure hunting. His father's pain is less important than his own fulfillment, and this leaves Biff in the difficult situation of trying to cope with personal defeat aggravated by paternal ruin. Biff shows genuine concern for the truth now that his illusions have been blasted away by Mr. Oliver. It will be this very need to expose the truth which will ultimately send Willy to his death, but Biff realizes that there can no longer be a life for him based on lies.

This is a dramatically complicated scene, and is more easily understood when seen on the stage. The stage directions specify different parts of the stage to be used for varying conflicts and chronological times. For example, the scenes with Miss Francis in Boston all take place on one part of the stage while the scenes in Frank's Chop House unravel on another. The spatial divisions make it easier to understand the flashbacks.

ACT II • SCENE 10

Summary

The Woman from Boston enters laughing, followed by Willy. There is a raw, sensuous atmosphere as he buttons his shirt. The knocking at the door continues and Willy answers it. Biff stands there with a suitcase and announces that he has let Willy down by flunking math. Biff relates the time when he was caught mimicking his teacher in front of the class. In the middle of his act, the teacher walked in. Miss Francis laughs from the bathroom and Biff asks if someone else is in the room. Then she comes out and Biff is horrified. Willy makes up a story about her room being painted ("so I let her take a shower here"), but he begins shouting at her to get out. She demands the two boxes of stockings which he had promised to her. Biff begins to cry and won't believe Willy's story, claiming that he gave the woman "Mama's stockings." He tells Willy he is a liar and a fake. Biff leaves the hotel room. Willy is on his knees on the floor. The time shifts back to the present as Willy shouts at Stanley the waiter, who helps him off the floor. Willy gives him his money and when Stanley refuses to take it, Willy adds: "Take it. You're a good boy. . . . Here — here's some more, I don't need it any more." Willy leaves, anxious to purchase some seeds at a hardware store.

Commentary

Willy's loneliness is underlined by his experience with Miss Francis in Boston. When Biff enters, he tells Willy about letting him down, and this serves to point out the extent to which Willy has let down his family. There is a parallel structure whereby Biff's teacher enters the classroom and catches Biff offguard in his satirical performance, and where Biff catches Willy offguard at the Standish Arms Hotel in Boston. This is the climax of the play since it is the point where Biff sees reality for the first time. It is also the moment when the most important person in Willy's life (Biff) is shattered by one of his actions. Life ceases to mean anything for Willy as of this experience, and everything goes downhill for Biff insofar as his future is concerned. Even Willy's betrayal of Linda is highlighted as he gives away "Mama's stockings". No one is sacred in Willy's life from this moment on, least of all himself. He is filled with a haunting despair over his infidelity, and his carelessness has led to the permanent rupture in his relationship with Biff.

Willy has just been fired and is at the low point in his life. The memories which flood his mind are matched only in intensity by the disappointment of Biff's encounter with Oliver. Everything converges at once in Willy's mind as he realizes his role in Biff's downfall. He is close to death but recalls that he has nothing to leave behind for his sons. This prompts him to go looking for seeds: "I've got to get some seeds right away. Nothing's planted. I don't have a thing in the ground." It is a scene for which Miller has very carefully prepared us and, from now on, it is only a matter of time before Willy's final act.

ACT II • SCENE 11

Summary
Biff and Happy arrive home later that evening with roses for Linda. She is not interested in flowers and demands to know where the two boys were when their father needed them. She orders them out of the house: "You're a pair of animals! Not one, not another living soul would have had the cruelty to walk out on that man in a restaurant!" Happy argues that Willy had a great time with them, but Biff tells him to shut up. Biff is filled with self-loathing. He sits on the floor in front of Linda and condemns himself for not having helped Willy: "Didn't do a damned thing. How do you like that, heh? Left him babbling in a toilet." While Happy has no accurate idea of himself, Biff knows he is "the scum of the earth." He determines to have an "abrupt conversation" with Willy when a hammering noise is heard outside the house: Willy is planting his garden.

Commentary
The importance of this scene is that Biff realizes he is worthless. When he attempts to make contact with his father in order to tell him this, he realizes the seriousness of Willy's condition. Planting a garden late at night is Willy's way of bringing things to a symbolic end. Biff is traumatized by this idea and can only reply: "Oh, my God!"

ACT II • SCENE 12

Summary
Willy is in the midst of planting seeds of various kinds. Ben

appears and moves slowly toward him. He converses with his brother about a "guaranteed twenty-thousand-dollar proposition," and reinforces the fact that Linda has suffered. It is a question of an insurance policy which Willy believes will bring Linda a great sum of money if he dies. Ben cautions that "they might not honor the policy." He tells Willy that suicide is cowardly. Willy fears that Biff thinks he is nothing, but a suicide will prove to the boy that his father was well liked everywhere. But Ben disagrees: Biff will hate Willy, call him a fool and view him as a coward. Willy, broken-hearted, wonders how one gets back to "all the great times." Ben glances at his watch and says he will consider Willy's proposition.

Commentary

This scene presents Willy's plan. He intends to kill himself so that his wife can collect a $20,000 insurance policy. Moreover, he wishes to prove to Biff that he is worth something and believes that death will bring him added credibility. In an effort to reach a decision, he has an imaginary conversation with Ben, who points out the disadvantages of suicide, but who also agrees that $20,000 "is something one can feel with the hand." It is ironical that Willy thinks Biff has been spiting him all his life, while Biff is anxious to confess his own inadequacies to his father. They are, at this point, leagues apart from understanding one another and will not be able to bridge the gap. Biff has moved closer to reality and Willy has milked his illusion to the point of death.

ACT II • SCENE 13

Summary

Willy notices Biff in the garden. He has come to say goodbye to his father and is not coming back any more. He tells Willy that there is no appointment with Oliver in the morning and that he doesn't want to fight with Willy as he usually has prior to leaving the Loman house. Biff is motivated by kindness, but Willy freezes, he does not wish to face his wife. Biff cannot understand this and places the blame on himself, not on Willy. Linda comes out and asks Willy if he has planted his seeds. Biff replies: "All right, we had it out. I'm going and I'm not writing any more." Linda is reconciled to this and states that the two men have never gotten along well. Biff tells Willy to put him right out of his life: "Forget I'm alive." Willy refuses to shake his hand and condemns him to rot in hell if he leaves the house. He accuses Biff of cutting down his own life for spite. Willy does not wish to be blamed for Biff's undoing. Biff is angered and produces the rubber hose, despite Linda's and Happy's protests. Biff feels no pity for his father.

Biff exposes Willy's lies and spares himself no pain in the process. He tells them about a jail term he spent in Kansas City and that he is a thief. He blames his behavior on Willy: "I never got anywhere because you blew me so full of hot air I could never stand taking orders from anybody! That's whose fault it is!" Linda attempts to stop Biff, but he is not finished. Biff realized earlier that day, while running down the stairs with the stolen fountain pen, that he did not need to steal any more. He knew what he loved about life and decided it was better than a life of illusion: "All I want is out there, waiting for me the minute I say I know who I am!" Biff is enraged with Willy and makes a move to attack him but is stopped by Happy. Biff's fury breaks down and he sobs, holding onto his father. Prophetically, Biff cries out to Willy: "Will you take that phony dream and burn it before something happens?" Biff goes upstairs and Willy is amazed that his son actually loves him: "Oh, Biff! He cried! Cried to me. That boy — that boy is going to be magnificent!"

Commentary

Biff is able, finally, to unburden his anger to Willy, but Willy fails to appreciate the significance of the interchange. For Biff, it is the beginning of a new life, one of honesty and straightforwardness, yet Willy insists to the end that Biff is going to become magnificent. Biff has no illusions about himself any more. He confesses to being a bum and exposes the crimes of his past as examples of his failure as a man. We discover that Biff has been a thief and has spent time in prison. He has traveled through seven states in an effort to make it big, but has failed every time. The episode of stealing the balls when he was an adolescent, cheating on exams in school and taking Mr. Oliver's pen that morning all point to the same thing. Biff has been searching for attention, for a way of re-arranging reality as he knows it and has believed it possible to take life on his own terms, regardless of the consequences. He now knows that this accomplishes nothing positive and he decides to abandon his lies for a more realistic life.

Biff is able to see Willy in a clearer light once he has understood himself more deeply. He realizes that his father is "a hard-working drummer who landed in the ash can like all the rest of them!" While his approach to Willy may not be gentle or kind, it is nonetheless grounded in honesty. The climax of the scene, Biff's crying, indicates that his conflict has exploded and he can now begin a new life.

ACT II • SCENE 14

Summary
Ben appears and indicates the $20,000 plan is a good one — Ben is something of a lure to the world of the dead. Happy repeats his plan to get married and to run the department store by the end of the year. He thereby furthers the illusion of success as taught him by Willy. Ben uses the metaphor of the jungle and the diamonds in order to urge Willy toward suicide. Willy sends Linda up to bed, and as she leaves, she says to him: "I think this is the only way, Willy," to which he replies: "Sure, it's the best thing." Willy is delighted about Biff's love for him and thinks $20,000 in his son's pocket would set him up for life. Ben sees it as a "perfect proposition all around." As Willy turns to leave the house, he utters one last speech of advice for Biff, instructing him to hit low and hard in the game. Linda calls to him, but Willy has rushed out of the house. A car is heard speeding off into the distance, and then it crashes.

Commentary
This is the scene of dénouement and it happens rapidly. Once Willy decides that Biff actually loves him, he is able to reconstruct his illusion of success wherein his son is dependent on him. The happiness he feels is intensified when he realizes that his suicide can bring Biff $20,000 and will make true success possible. Willy is proud that Biff will be ahead of Bernard again.

Ben represents the force which lures Willy toward death — that is, toward the act of killing himself. But when Ben disappears from the scene, Willy is afraid and becomes panicky. At this point, he is surrounded with sounds, faces and voices which torment him. They are enough to drive him out of the house and into his car, the suicide weapon. It is ironical that Willy actually drives himself to death, literally and figuratively. Another aspect of irony is brought out in Willy's last words with Linda. She says to him: "I think this is the only way" and no doubt is referring to the fact that Biff must leave the house. Willy's reply is: "Sure, it's the best thing," again in the sense of Biff and his separation being a positive step for both of them. But on a deeper level, Linda's words can be seen as an eery premonition of Willy's death, and Willy's response is a suitable summary of all he has been through. Without realizing it, he has signed his own death warrant; it has been a gradual process, but he now has no alternative.

REQUIEM

Summary

At the grave a few days later, Linda wonders why no one has come to the funeral. She explains to Charley that it was the first time in 35 years that their debts were almost entirely paid, and that all Willy would have needed was a little salary. Charley replies with: "No man only needs a little salary." Biff reminisces about the happy times with Willy: building a front porch, adding a bathroom to the house and so on. He claims Willy had all the wrong dreams and Happy prepares himself to fight his brother for saying this. Charley settles the matter by interpreting the essence of a salesman's soul: "A salesman is got to dream, boy. It comes with the territory."

Linda asks to be left alone so that she can say good-bye to Willy. She is unable to cry and cannot understand why he killed himself. The play ends in an emotional sweep as Linda addresses Willy directly: "I made the last payment on the house today. Today, dear. And there'll be nobody home. We're free and clear. We're free. We're free . . . We're free . . ."

Commentary

As might have been expected, no one came to Willy's funeral. He was not the important man he deemed himself to be — at least, not in the eyes of his business associates and acquaintances.

Happy is angry with Biff for making statements about

Willy's futile dreams. This is because Happy has not yet accepted the nature of Willy's illusion and does not wish to see his fantasy world crumble. Biff knows the truth, but Happy vows to "win it for him [i.e. Willy]." While there is some semblance of hope for Biff, there is no indication of change in Happy. His values have remained the same and his life will probably continue in the same direction. He is an excellent candidate for becoming the new Willy Loman.

Linda is the tragic figure in this last scene. She has been patient, kind and loving with her husband, and now she is alone. Her sons have their own lives and she is without the challenge of looking after her husband. Paying off the mortgage is, symbolically, her way of saying that she is no longer indebted to anyone, including Willy. She is free from the pain and can at least begin to put things in perspective. She ends the play on a note of sadness, but there is nonetheless optimism in her "We're free."

The drama ends as the stage darkens and the house is dwarfed by the towers of the nearby apartment buildings.

Character Sketches

Willy Loman

Willy's last name is a pun on the words "low man." He is at the bottom of the social and economic ladder in a highly competitive society. He owns nothing and he produces nothing.

Because of his social status, Willy clings to a theory of personal attractiveness. He believes that one's popularity and handsomeness determine how successful one will be in life. As support for this belief, Willy refers to Dave Singleman, who was so popular and such a successful salesman that when he died people came from all over the United States to attend his funeral. Willy was committed to duplicating the personal successes of Singleman.

But, by the time we meet Willy, he is not popular and he is no longer attractive. He is incapable of doing a good job at selling, but he is unwilling to admit his failure. His imagination and deceit take over, allowing him to tell his wife that he is very successful and extremely popular. Still, he has his doubts and these are expressed occasionally.

The lies he tells entrap him. Not only is his failure humiliating, it also makes him face the dishonesty with which he has lived his life. He is extremely vulnerable to loneliness. Thus, a traveling job does not mesh very well with his attitudes.

Consequently, Willy had to escape from his trap. He did this in two ways: imaginary returns to the past, and his eventual suicide. The suicide is precipitated by the increasingly disconcerting nature of his daydreams. He becomes disoriented and cannot find any pleasure in his reminiscing.

Biff says that Willy is a fake and so are his dreams. This is a key to Willy. His ideas concerning personal attractiveness are paramount in his life, and they fail him miserably as he grows older and his son, Biff, fails in life.

There is not much to like in Willy, but there is much to pity. Willy has few characteristics that could be called likeable. We only pity him for the situation he is in. He is old, gruff and flighty. He refuses to accept his own limitations.

Miller has said that Willy personifies any man, great or small, who risks everything to retain his own identity. But Willy had mistaken his identity. He assumed a character other than his true one. He sacrificed himself to the great gods, Popularity and Success. What the salesman was attempting to sell, it would seem, was himself.

Willy is Everyman. He faces all the decisions and temptations that the hero of the classic morality play faced. He arouses contempt, pity, fear and anger. He makes us question common assumptions. Miller says that Willy is searching for the "right way to live so that the world is a home."

Linda Loman

Linda Loman's entire life revolves around her husband. She is always willing to believe Willy and ceaselessly support him. Therein lies her greatest weakness.

Of all people, Linda had the strength to bring Willy out of his illusory world and back to reality, but she fails to utilize this. Linda has little personal initiative and would rather be led than disturb matters.

As a somewhat biased wife, Linda must share the blame for the downfall of Willy Loman. On those rare occasions when Willy would attempt to look at himself honestly, Linda would disclaim his realistic observations and reinforce his incorrect attitudes. In her reluctance to accept Willy's failures, she is as incorrigible as he is.

But on the other side of this, we find that Linda is a very faithful wife. She defends Willy to his sons and demands that "attention, attention must finally be paid to this man." To the end, she is a solace to Willy, though he often treats her with something less than respect.

But, as a character, Linda's role in the play is not so complex. She is a simple person who cannot bring herself to act when she must do so. When she realizes that Willy has been contemplating suicide, she does not really face the problem and try to discuss it with him.

Biff Loman

Biff Loman is Willy's elder son and is more complicated than his brother, Happy. Biff has always been favored by Willy as a young man with enormous potential in life. In high school he was a brilliant football player and was offered numerous scholarships to college. Yet his progress in school came to a halt when he experienced first-hand the extra-marital affair of his father with Miss Francis. This drove him to squander the gains he had made in life and give up trying to become someone important. Biff was shocked into turmoil by Willy's affair, and the transformation he undergoes in this play traces, indirectly, the path of frustration which he has led until the present.

After leaving high school, Biff spent many years traveling from state to state in search of his identity. He had stolen a ball when he was in high school, and this pattern of thievery continued into his early adult years. He confesses late in the play that he spent time in prison for having stolen property from others. Biff has suffered deep anxiety since losing respect for his father and bounces back and forth in his quest for values, for self-esteem. Willy had always been his role model, his ideal father, but when Biff realized that the man had serious flaws in his personality — that he was human and not superhuman — he was unable to tolerate his father's belief system. An essential aspect of the play is the development of Biff Loman from the stage of *knowing* that he and Willy are fakes to *telling* himself and his father that this is the case. Biff is unable to play Willy's game any longer and confronts him with his convictions. Though Willy cannot bear to hear anything other than success, talent and excellence from his son, Biff proceeds nonetheless to fulfill his inner urges for truth. He exposes his feelings and forces the issue with Willy. The confrontation is so intense that it leaves him in tears, sobbing; he is unburdened of his misery and can begin to see life differently, with hope. He is in a position to learn from Willy's errors and plan for the future with more realism. He knows that a man cannot live by the values of his father, that every person needs to have a unique set of beliefs. Perhaps more important than any of his discoveries is the fact that Biff sees how personal attractiveness means little if it is only skin-deep. Truth and integrity take place on a more fundamental level and cannot be glossed over by good looks or illusions of success.

Biff is the character who represents positive growth whereas his brother Happy resolves to continue Willy's system of beliefs. Biff, therefore, is the one of whom Willy would no doubt be the most proud since, in the long run, his outlook on life stands to bring him more success than Happy's.

Happy Loman
Happy had always been overshadowed by his older brother,

Biff. Consequently, he develops a need for recognition, which is characterized by his comments that he is losing weight and that he is considering getting married.

By the end of the play we are aware that Willy has little time for Happy and has always considered him second to Biff. This rejection is reciprocated in the restaurant scene when Happy tells the two girls he has picked up that Willy is not his father, "He's just a guy." Happy may have been justified in doing this, since Willy had paid little attention to him all his life.

Happy is not a very deep character. As his name implies, he is a "good-time guy." Not only is he a proficient liar, he also lacks any real personal ethics. He is waiting for his boss to die so he can be promoted. As such, he represents the very worst of Willy's character.

He is not an admirable person. At the close of the play, Biff gains enlightenment, but Happy is more blind than ever. He mires himself in Willy's values, saying that he will struggle to take up where Willy left off. Thus, Happy is an appropriate foil to the newly awakened Biff.

Charley

Charley is the next-door neighbor of Willy and Linda Loman. He has been close to their family for many years and his son, Bernard, grew up with Biff Loman. Because of this closeness, the boys called him Uncle Charley, even though there is no blood relationship.

Charley is a practical, emotionally secure man whose success in life came from a careful, cautious approach. He is offered in contrast to the energetic, 'big time' Willy Loman, whose idea of success has no basis in reality. Charley is not a dreamer. He is a systematic, objective sort of person who looks at each obstacle in life as an isolated incident to be examined unemotionally. Clearly he is the antithesis of Willy Loman.

Charley is not "well liked," to use Willy's term, but this does not matter to him. Outer appearances are of little importance to Charley since his is a life of quiet organization. He is neither a snob nor a bore, but enjoys playing cards, socializing with his neighbors and upholding the basic values in his life. Whereas Willy thinks it is important to be personally attractive, Charley pays no attention to this; his success proves that there are ways other than Willy's of looking at life. It is Charley's success that annoys Willy and which prevents the latter from accepting employment from his friend when Charley offers it. But Charley continues to lend him money although he feels insulted by Willy's refusal to work for him. Thus, we can see the benevolent side of his character.

Charley is a man of few words and speaks his mind only when provoked. Sometimes his anger toward Willy is expressed in the form of questions, such as: "When are you going to grow up?" He knows that Willy has certain talents, motivation and energy, but he also understands what it takes to succeed in life — and Willy lacks this sensible, practical knowledge.

Charley is, by nature, a down-to-earth, realistic character whose function is to show by contrast the exaggerations of Willy's illusion. At the end of the play, during the Requiem, he summarizes Willy's character by saying that the man was a salesman, and as such, needed to dream. Charley lends emotional support to Linda and brings Willy Loman into a more favorable light, showing him as a man with faults but also with a heart.

Ben

Ben is a shadowy figure who functions more as a symbol or illusion than he does as a character. What we see of Ben, as a character, is not necessarily favorable from a purely objective view. He does not believe at all in the moral strength of the individual and he tells Biff never to fight fair with a stranger. His success seems to have been built on brute force and driving energy. He has no time for personal relations, nor does he seem to indulge in emotions. But the reader should remember that these qualities are conjecture, and we see Ben only through Willy's eyes. In fact, if Charley had not asked about Ben, and if Linda had not reminded Willy that he sold the diamond watch he received from Ben, the reader could well wonder whether Ben had ever lived.

But the above qualities assigned to Ben serve to reinforce his function in the play. He is the ideal for Willy, even though, ironically, he is also the antithesis of Willy. For Willy, Ben represents the ideal success story. He entered the "jungle" when he was 17, and when he came out at 21 he was rich. He achieved the complete success that Willy can only dream about.

Ben is diametrically opposed to Charley, who is the practical man who has attained a limited degree of success; the former represents unbridled enterprise, while the latter succeeds through plodding acquiescence. Because Charley lived next door to Willy, Charley's success is that much more repugnant to Willy. While Ben, who has remained far away, is the far-removed and romanticized success story.

Ben also functions as a character who Willy can rely upon in a moment of extreme depression. Ben becomes, therefore, Willy's psychological "crutch." When Willy can't face the pressing problems of the world, he talks with Ben: the symbol of perfect success. Therefore, Ben functions mainly, not as a character, but as a symbol that illuminates an aspect of Willy's frustrations.

Literary Elements

Plot

The plot of this play is simple, straightforward and without complication. Miller is not a dramatist who weaves intricate stories or who enjoys creating confusion in the plot line. Rather, he focuses on dramatic tension and involves the spectator/reader in a world of deep, churning emotions. Basically, the plot of *Death of a Salesman* is this: Willy Loman, a salesman, has spent his life in a dream world pursuing a goal which he will never achieve. His two sons conflict with each other, one attempting to keep Willy on his path of destruction, the other trying to free his father with the truth. His wife Linda provides a steadying influence to this conflict as she gropes for ways of bringing balance back into Willy's life.

Theme

There are various themes at work here. The theme of success is the underriding guide to the action. Willy has a notion of success which he has never been able to achieve. He believes in superlatives: the best, the most, the finest, the brightest. His vision of Biff is not in keeping with the reality of his son's existence, but is based on an illusion founded years earlier when the boy was in his youth. Willy's idea of success is, ironically, the agent which brings about his failure in the end. He has an unrealistic approach to solving problems, preferring the quick and simple method of closing his eyes to all conflict.

The theme of love is also explored. It is manifested in an entangled manner throughout the numerous relationships in the play. Linda exhibits an unquestioning, dedicated love for her husband and even for her sons, though she resents the boys' inability to 'get along with' their father. The two sons, in their own way, love their father. Happy lives in the same town as the Lomans and has seen Willy's development from a closer standpoint. He urges his brother to take more of an interest in the man, but Biff soon realizes (after the theft of Mr. Oliver's fountain pen), that his love can only be fulfilled if he is truthful with his father. Biff's great love is shown when he explodes at Willy in Act II and tells him the truth about themselves.

There is even a certain love in the friendship between Charley and Willy, although Willy would perhaps never have admitted to it. They have been friends for years and Willy depends on Charley, in his last months of life, for his financial support. Charley shows compassion and patience with Willy, well beyond what most people have shown him. He is there right to the end and helps Linda through the pain of Willy's death.

Structure

In terms of the play's dramatic structure, we are dealing with a brilliantly conceived and executed work of drama which plays with our concept of time through the use of flashback and intricate staging. Miller has stated that "the ultimate matter with which the play will close is announced at the outset and is the matter of its every moment from the first." The plot is not developed chronologically, but rather in a bit-by-bit piecing together of events. The play begins in the present as Willy is shown in the grips of his conflict. We do not yet know what has preceded this crisis situation, but Miller tells us what we need to understand through a series of flashbacks and daydreaming sequences. We soon discover that Willy's lack of self-worth derives from experiences related to his son Biff, to his waning career as a salesman and to his inability to make life wonderful for his wife Linda. It is the story of an aging man who considers himself a failure but is incapable of consciously admitting it. His debts prey on him like so many chains and daggers and he reaches the point where everything seems to break down before it is "paid for." Through a process of zig-zagging that spans the past, present and future, Miller presents his central character in the midst of a crisis which he resolves through suicide. The reality of his problems are too much to bear and he seeks a solution in death. The setting varies from Willy's house to Charley's office, Ebbets Football Field, Frank's Chop House and the hotel in Boston, but most important is the inner mind of Willy Loman: it is there that one must see the action unravel since the drama lies not so much in certain events but in Willy's perception and recollection of those events.

The drama takes place in two Acts without specific scene divisions. Miller has created two blocks of drama within one play, separated by an intermission, and the intensity of emotion reached is considerable. Since all of the action leads to the resolution of the crisis, there is a constant pounding away of tension, conflict, emotion and human passion. Each word spoken is necessary and carries layers of meaning which contribute to the work as a whole.

Language and Style

The language used by Miller is beautiful in both its poetic nuance and its gripping realism. The playwright spares no violence or emotion in his efforts to capture the precise feeling of the moment. It is the language and the merry-go-round effect of words plastered onto words which accomplishes the spinning sensation of scenes such as the one where Biff discovers his father in the hotel room with Miss Francis.

The full title of the play is: *Death of a Salesman: Certain Private Conversations in Two Acts and a Requiem*. This tells us something important about the style involved. It is intimate, free-flowing and conversational in tone. Miller uses the dramatic form to excite the voyeurism in his spectators. They are privy to information which would ordinarily be considered "private conversations" between members of the Loman family. Without the pretense of social facades, the characters are able to express themselves with candor, honesty and spontaneity. These are arguments which they have had for many years and which are close to the surface. This facilitates the eventual clash which occurs at the end of Act II and which leads to such harsh words as those exchanged between Biff and Willy. When father tells son: "You vengeful, spiteful mutt," we understand immediately what is behind this intense condemnation. Taken out of context, this speech would seem somewhat unbelievable and would reflect badly on the speaker. But we know what is happening inside Willy's mind and we accept the fact that he is desperate, that he has no further recourse but to attack the person he loves most in life.

This kind of dramatic tension is achieved through swift dialogue, simple language, direct expression of thought and highly manipulated psychological conflict. This is reinforced by the language of the setting, a non-verbal but always present arena in which the spoken word rebounds, clatters, echoes and tantalizes:

The entire setting is wholly or, in some places, partially transparent. The roof-line of the house is one-dimensional; under and over it we see the apartment

61

buildings. Before the house lies an apron, curving beyond the forestage into the orchestra. This forward area serves as the back yard as well as the locale of all Willy's imaginings and of his city scenes. Whenever the action is in the present the actors observe the imaginary wall-lines, entering the house only through its door . . . . But in the scenes of the past these boundaries are broken, and characters enter to leave a room by stepping "through" a wall onto the forestage.

(Act I, Intro.)

The intracacies of setting his drama on this kind of stage allows Miller to shift the focus from external realism to psychological realism. The interest of the drama is psychological and is reinforced through the tightness of the locale. The setting speaks indirectly to our unconscious, especially when we see the play on stage as opposed to in text form. A stifling atmosphere can be created through use of walls which close in on the characters, and this feeling is even expressed by Willy as he laments the arrival of tall apartment buildings which hem them in.

There is also a language of time, alongside that of space (i.e. setting). Miller sweeps back and forth from past to present to past, and creates an inescapable carnival of mental anguish as his character falls prey to his own mind. When a present situation provokes the memory or nostalgia of a past event, Willy is jarred into reliving his past, regardless of its nature — sometimes pleasant, often traumatic, always significant. When Willy stumbles in confusion at Frank's Chop House, there is a parallel to his emotional inebriation and confusion in addition to the swirling pattern of his life. Nothing is in vain in this play. Every moment, word or action plays a vital role in the fabric of Willy's drama. Time, setting, psychological intention and spoken language are all woven together to show the pattern of Willy's life.

Symbolism and Imagery

Symbolism prevails throughout the play. There are examples in almost every scene. The stockings which Linda darns and which Willy presents as a gift to Miss Francis are a symbol of Willy's career, his self-worth, his 'product'. At home, his life is in a crisis situation and the stockings are full of holes. Linda, the proverbial loving wife, attempts to mend their life as she symbolically mends holes in the stockings. Willy is enraged at her darning and orders her to throw the stockings in the garbage. This is symbolic of his desire to be free of problems at home and enjoy a life of success and harmony. When Biff discovers his father with Miss Francis, he pounces upon the fact that Willy has given her "Mama's stockings." Again, the garments represent a bond of integrity and happiness which has been violated, and Biff holds this against his father.

The car plays a symbolic role in the sense that Willy, quite literally, drives himself to death. We learn from Linda that Willy has staged several previous car accidents, perhaps early attempts to commit suicide, but certainly ways of drawing attention to his condition. The car represents power, movement forward, acceleration and mobility — all of which are symbols in Willy's life of hopelessness, decay and despair. It comes as no surprise that he chooses this vehicle as an instrument with which to kill himself.

The fountain pen which Biff steals is symbolic as the focal point of Biff's inadequacies. He has no need for the pen, nor is it meaningful in any unconscious manner. Rather, it serves to highlight the absurdity of theft, the demeaning quality of taking from someone something which you do not need. Biff has lived a life based on Willy's values, but when he discovers that these values are not good for him, he abandons them in search of his own. The pen can be seen as the symbol of someone else's values, of someone else's possessions. Biff discards them in favor of integrity and belief in himself. He wishes to get rid of his life-long habit of taking from others (e.g. the ball back in high school). He has spent time in prison, and this represents symbolically the time he has spent imprisoned by his father's mentality.

At the play's end, Willy purchases some seeds for his garden and begins to plant them late at night. He is close to suicide but realizes that he must leave something tangible behind as a legacy for his sons. Again, it is symbolic of his desire to grow big and tall, and will be harvested in the form of Biff's new attitudes toward life. Biff is the one who will secure growth in life. Happy, in his determination to continue Willy's action, can be seen as the weed in the Loman's garden.

In terms of imagery, the most important is that of "the

woods are burning." Willy's brother Ben made a success of himself early in life and compared the process of success-building to entering a jungle: "When I was seventeen, I walked into the jungle and when I was twenty-one I walked out . . . . And by God I was rich." The jungle is seen as the locale of Ben's success, but for Willy, the forest is burning, there is little time left, the world has devoured him like so many flames and left only the ashes of a man with dreams. When Willy is angered with his son Happy, who wishes to retire his father for life, Willy knows only too well that he has little life left to him: "The woods are burning. I can't even drive a car." This image is symbolic of Willy's feeling that everything is closing in on him: time, debts, human relationships. Even the apartment buildings in his neighborhood are closing in on him and he cannot bear the pressures. That is why ultimately he throws himself into the fire and commits suicide.

Critical Appraisal

When all is said and done, *Death of a Salesman* will remain one of the great American tragedies of the 20th century. Much has been written on the question of whether "tragedy" is the legitimate category into which this play should be filed. Some claim that there is no resemblance between the action and characters of this drama and the great figures required by pure tragedy (e.g. kings, queens, nobles, impressive people). Miller has argued against these criticisms, stating his belief that the play is indeed a tragedy. To be sure, it is tragic that a man can live his life within the confines of an illusion, and realize at the conclusion of his career that his values have amounted to nothing, that he is not even close to achieving his goals. Whether we choose the term "tragedy" seems less important than our ability to interpret the tragic nature of Loman's life.

One of the more important questions addressed in this play is that of success and its meaning. Success is a state of mind and has nothing to do with material trappings, money and social prestige. One can be successful, according to one's own definition of success, without any of these external possessions. But the latter can play a large role in achieving success if this is all that a person deems important. Willy Loman has created a system in which to live and it is based on his notion of personal attractiveness. He believes that the outer self is what people enjoy and that attractiveness is the important force in determining success. We see throughout the play that he is not admired by others, that he lacks this attractiveness, and that, by his own definition, he can never become a success. Biff, on the other hand, is the handsome football player gifted with personal attractiveness but who is unable to use this to achieve goals. Perhaps this is because he *has* no goals. He believes that everything will eventually happen for him, that effort, planning, organization and hard work are not necessary when one is "personally attractive." He has inherited this belief from Willy, but by the play's end realizes that one must do more in life than pay lip-service to empty notions. Everyone aspires to success and most people have dreamed about having more money in their pockets. But Miller's message is loud and clear on this subject: one must define what is truthful and real about one's personality and goals, and then measure success by what can realistically be achieved. This does not exclude the process of dreaming, earning large sums of money and attaining social status, but it does imply the need for realistic assessment of the self. This is the area of Willy Loman's greatest failure.

Death of a Salesman is significant because its drama is deeply human. Everyone who reads or sees this play has experienced some of the emotions contained therein, and we all identify with the frustrations of Willy's condition. The play's appeal, from this standpoint, is universal and can be appreciated in translation anywhere in the world. There is no shortage of critical reaction to Miller's drama, but more important than individual critic's ideas is the awareness in each person that the play can be approached from an independent, personal stance. Each reader should develop his or her own reactions to the drama and attempt to understand why such feelings are present. For as Miller has said: "A playwright provides answers by the questions he chooses to ask." These questions are valid for each of us, and the value of reading plays such as *Death of a Salesman* lies in their ability to help us understand ourselves as human beings.

*Arthur Miller on *Death of a Salesman*

Experience tells me that I will probably know better next year what I feel right now about the first anniversary of "Death of a Salesman"—it usually takes that long to understand anything. I suppose I ought to try to open some insights into the play. Frankly, however, it comes very fuzzily to mind at this date. I have not sat through it since dress rehearsal and haven't read it since the proofs went to the publisher. In fact, it may well be that from the moment I read it to my wife and two friends one evening in the country a year ago last fall, the play cut itself off from me in a way that is incomprehensible.

I remember that night clearly, best of all. The feeling of disaster when, glancing up at the audience of three, I saw nothing but glazed looks in their eyes. And at the end, when they said nothing, the script suddenly seemed a record of a madness I had passed through, something I ought not admit to at all, let alone read aloud or have produced on the stage.

I don't remember what they said, exactly, excepting that it had taken them deeply. But I can see my wife's eyes as I read a—to me—a hilarious scene, which I prefer not to identify. She was weeping. I confess that I laughed more during the writing of this play than I have ever done, when alone, in my life. I laughed because moment after moment came when I felt I had rapped it right on the head—the non sequitur, the aberrant but meaningful idea racing through Willy's head, the turn of story that kept surprising me every morning. And most of all the form, for which I have been searching since the beginning of my writing life.

Writing in that form was like moving through a corridor in a dream, knowing instinctively that one would find every wriggle of it and, best of all, where the exit lay. There is something like a dream's quality in my memory of the writing and the day or two that followed its completion.

I remember the rehearsal when we had our first audience. Six or seven friends. The play working itself out under the single bulb overhead. I think that was the first and only time I saw it as others see it. Then it seemed to me that we must be a terribly lonely people, cut off from each other by such massive pretense

*Editor's title. From "The 'Salesman' Has a Birthday," *The New York Times*, February 5, 1950, II, pp. 1-3.

of self-sufficiency, machined down so fine we hardly touch any more. We are trying to save ourselves separately, and that is immoral, that is the corrosive among us.

On that afternoon, more than any time before or since, the marvel of the actor was all new to me. How utterly they believed what they were saying to each other!

To watch fine actors creating their roles is to see revealed the innocence, the naïve imagination of man liberated from the prisons of the past. They were like children wanting to show that they could turn themselves into anybody, thus opening their lives to limitless possibilities.

And Elia Kazan, with his marvelous wiles, tripping the latches of the secret little doors that lead into the always different personalities of each actor. That is his secret; not merely to know what must be done, but to know the way to implement the doing for actors trained in diametrically opposite schools, or not trained at all. He does not "direct," he creates a center point, and then goes to each actor and creates the desire to move toward it. And they all meet, but for different reasons, and seem to have arrived there by themselves.

Was there ever a production of so serious a play that was carried through with so much exhilarating laughter? I doubt it. We were always on the way, and I suppose we always knew it.

There are things learned—I think, by many people—from this production. Things which, if applied, can bring much vitality to our theatre.

There is no limit to the expansion of the audience imagination so long as the play's internal logic is kept inviolate. It is not true that conventionalism is demanded. They will move with you anywhere, they will believe right into the moon so long as you believe who tell them this tale. We are at the beginning of many explosions of form. They are waiting for wonders.

A serious theme is entertaining to the extent that it is not trifled with, not cleverly angled, but met in head-on collision. They will not consent to suffer while the creators stand by with tongue in cheek. They have a way of knowing. Nobody can blame them.

And there have been certain disappointments, one above all. I am sorry the self-realization of the older son, Biff, is not a weightier counterbalance to Willy's disaster in the audience mind.

68

And certain things more clearly known, or so it seems now. We want to give of ourselves, and yet all we train for is to take, as though nothing less will keep the world at a safe distance. Every day we contradict our will to create, which is to give. The end of man is not security, but without security we are without the elementary condition of humaneness.

A time will come when they will look back at us astonished that we saw something holy in the competition for the means of existence. But already we are beginning to ask of the great man, not what has he got, but what has he done for the world. We ought to be struggling for a world in which it will be possible to lay blame. Only then will the great tragedies be written, for where no order is believed in, no order can be breached, and thus all disasters of man will strive vainly for moral meaning.

And what have such thoughts to do with this sort of reminiscence? Only that to me the tragedy of Willy Loman is that he gave his life, or sold it, in order to justify the waste of it. It is the tragedy of a man who did believe that he alone was not meeting the qualifications laid down for mankind by those clean-shaven frontiersmen who inhabit the peaks of broadcasting and advertising offices. From those forests of canned goods high up near the sky, he heard the thundering command to succeed as it ricocheted down the newspaper-lined canyons of his city, heard not a human voice, but a wind of a voice to which no human can reply in kind, except to stare into the mirror at a failure.

So what is there to feel on this anniversary? Hope, for I know now that the people want to listen. A little fear that they want to listen so badly. And an old insistence—sometimes difficult to summon, but there none the less—that we will find a way beyond fear of each other, beyond bellicosity, a way into our humanity.

Death of a Salesman, Contemporary Tragedy*

Unlike the dramas by Sophocles, Shakespeare, and Lorca, Arthur Miller's *Death of a Salesman* is a tragedy set in our own times, played out on our own scene, by characters who, however we regard the quality of their thought, speak in our own language and with our own peculiar accents. In one sense, therefore, we cannot claim that the play is foreign to us. For what we lose of *Oedipus* because we are not Athenians, and of *Othello* because we are not Elizabethans, and of *Blood Wedding* by not being Spaniards, that much, at least, is ours because we are Miller's American contemporaries. Even were we to reject his assumptions and deny his conclusions, we would still know the world Miller creates, because the apartment houses that cut off Willy's horizon cut off our own as well, and the three thousand miles from Brooklyn to San Francisco involve more a change of name and site than of setting.

Centering on the quality of the protagonist, most of the comment about this play has argued the question of whether Willy Loman has sufficient stature to be a tragic hero. There is an irony in this debate over the admission of Willy to the company of Oedipus and Othello: few commentators have recognized the significance of the play's structure, of its use of scenes that embody and, at the same time, illustrate the insubstantiality of the salesman's world of the smile and backslap; for the chosen structure indicates that Willy, though no less heroic—no less committed, that is, to his own dreams—is cast in a different mold than that used for the traditional hero. We begin, therefore, with what is most notable about the structure of the play itself, its treatment of time.

As in all tragedies, we first meet the hero a few moments before his end. But Miller's drama does not rely on the usual compressed expository report to acquaint us with the antecedent action necessary to an understanding of the hero's motives. Partly because the advance of modern psychology has made it easy for us to shift from the present to its root-experience in the past and back again, and partly because an illusion of such

*Editor's title. From *The Dramatic Experience* by Judah Bierman, James Hart and Stanley Johnson (Englewood Cliffs, N.J.: Prentice-Hall, 1958), pp. 490-493.

movement lies within the technical capacity of the modern stage, Miller has chosen actually to show us the scenes which made up the life that now dissolves before us. These he shows us as they exist in Willy's mind, that is, without any clear distinction as to the particular times at which they happened. Thus we come to witness, and not simply to know by report, the younger life of Willy Loman, who, some thirty-five years before, started his pilgrimage to the grave we now stand beside with his wife Linda, and his boys, Biff and Happy. This treatment of time, by putting emphasis on the earlier scenes, reduces the impact of the final suicide. On the other hand, it serves to raise that suicide to the level of sacrifice by linking it with Willy's early dreams.

Into his visualization of the last forty-eight hours of the hero's life, Miller introduces two other kinds of scenes: those involving guidance from Ben, and those involving the nurture of Biff. The first kind are objectifications of Willy's own insecurity, for Willy bows down to the image of Ben's success, finding in Ben's words—as in those of a Delphic oracle—both a guide for action and a reassurance that his own ideas are right. And the second kind of scene shows us Willy bending his son's knee before the idol of success, teaching him the liturgy of the smile, and making him to believe that over the door of heaven is inscribed: "Enter here only the well-liked." These scenes (and that other visualization of the past, the episode of the Woman in Boston), give dimension to the portrait of the protagonist. Without them, the play's theme-statements would be what they are sometimes unwittingly taken to be: sentimental idealizations of a failure. With them, it becomes clear that Willy's failure stems from the quality of his aspirations, and not of his spirit.

> I don't say he's a great man. Willy Loman never made a lot of money. His name was never in the paper. He's not the finest character that ever lived. But he's a human being, and a terrible thing is happening to him. So attention must be paid. He's not to be allowed to fall into his grave like an old dog. Attention, attention must be finally paid to such a person.

The second is the epitaph that Charlie reads over his friend, Willy Loman—salesman, sixty-three, suspected suicide:

Nobody dast blame this man. You don't understand: Willy was a salesman. And for a salesman, there is no rock bottom to the life. He don't put a bolt to a nut, he don't tell you the law or give you medicine. He's a man way out there in the blue.

Now, in the first statement, Linda argues that Willy Loman, because he is a man, must have what all men must have: if his name is not to be written in the permanent records of Man, he must at least be able to hear the voices of his children. This minimal certificate of immortality he must have to keep him from oblivion. But Charlie, on the other hand, speaks of Willie as a salesman, not as a human being. There are men, he says, whose lives are built of necessity on nothing more substantial than the smile and the shine, whose satisfactions are no more enduring than dreams of bigger and still bigger orders. A man such as these cannot be blamed for his action if he chooses to die "dramatically" in a last attempt to gain for himself a more substantial place in the memory of men. Some commentators have in effect combined the two theme-statements, asserting that what Miller intended was an indictment of the American system for ruthlessly discarding its faithful servants. For them, Willy symbolizes the failure of the American capitalist ethos, its basic destruction of the humanity of man.

Each of these interpretations—the wife's, the friend's, and the critical view that combines them—points toward the meaning of the play, but each also raises questions that it leaves unanswered. Can we, for example, accept Linda's demand that "attention be paid," knowing as we do the shallowness of Willy's past? Does not this knowledge degrade him below the level of interest? Plain souls like this salesman are of interest to their families and to God; but we need greatness to inspire us. On the other hand, if Miller's concern lay with the tragedy of a salesman in a capitalist world, why did he not show us at least a successful salesman? Willy succeeds only with his batch of cement; he is a carpenter and a planter. But as a salesman he is a failure. Can he then be a valid symbol in an indictment of the capitalist world? Is he more than a symbol of failure?

These questions emphasize the danger, particularly acute in tragedy, of confusing the poetic statement with the whole meaning of the play; life as revealed in tragedy cannot be so easily summed up in a line or two of dialogue. The keys to meaning, on the contrary, are found in the plot, in the characters, and in the conflict that engages them. The conflict Miller chose to communicate his vision is that between Willy as a salesman and Willy as a man. Such a view of the conflict explains and justifies the author's uses of the past; each of the episodes can now be seen as making the same, insistent point: Willy suffers from his attempt to live by his business ethics. He is content to govern all his relationships, including those with his family, by the same standards that prevail when he is on the road. He cannot distinguish—as we do, and as the play insists we do—between the ethics of business (a little happy cheating now and then) and the sterner ethics of life.

Willy is blind to the fundamental contradiction between his progress as a salesman and his self-realization as a man, and his blindness is almost allegorically reflected in his children. Like Willy, Happy lives the life of the business ethic. Like his father, he fails to understand that the smile is no safe-conduct pass through the jungle. Significantly, he is incapable of fruition; he is a philanderer, and wastes himself in a succession of casual, fruitless unions. He has the smell of women on him, in a play in which men cry out to assert their masculinity. Biff, on the other hand, reflects Willy's discontent. He does not understand what troubles him: who his father is. And the episode of the Woman in Boston sets him adrift because the episode is a combined revelation of Willy's key to successful selling and his recurrent attempts to blot out his feelings of inconsequentiality. Biff comes home and is symbolically set free only when he discovers himself as a nobody.

The whole question of Willy's hidden identity is curiously like that in *Oedipus*. The key words—he does not know who he is—point the parallel almost unmistakably. But before we rank the salesman with the king, we need to check one further structural element. From Aristotle to Maxwell Anderson the point of *recognition* has been fundamental in the structure of tragedy. Biff, as we have seen, finally recognizes his situation; he reports that in his flight with the pen, he has suddenly realized the falsity of his life. He discovers his own identity, even though he identifies himself as a nobody. But where is Willy's moment of recognition, and what does it amount to? How much does Willy really see, even after that climactic scene in which Biff, tendering his love, frees both himself and his father? The question we are really asking is whether Willy Loman recognizes anything equal in quality to that which drove Oedipus to his self-mutilation and Othello to his suicide. The answer is both yes and no.

The *impact* of his recognition is of equal quality: it drives him to decisive action. What is different and debased is the quality of the action taken, the solution envisioned. Unable to rise above the commercial values that have defined and limited his life, Willy comes to suicide only as a new answer to his old problem. He is giving Biff something in return for his tendered love; he will trade himself for the money which he still sees as the key to his son's success in life. What is debased is Willy's immature evaluation, and the equally immature response founded on it. It is the response of a man who chooses death, not because life has been made intolerable by a terrible burden of guilt, but because he believes that his death is the purchase price of a security he himself could never find.

But perhaps the best approach to Willy's place among tragic heroes is to ask of his death the same class of question that we ask of the others. Concerning the fall of Oedipus, ruler of Thebes, solver of the Sphinx's riddle, we ask, "Does this fall mean that man is driven by an insatiable desire to know (above all to know himself), but, at the same time, that this desire for self-knowledge leads ultimately to blindness and destruction?" As we witness the fall of Othello, prince of Moors, General of Venice, Governor of Cyprus, we ask, "Does this fall mean that we have in us all that seed of jealousy which, given a dark moment of despair, will germinate and flower into a passion that destroys all reason?" And of the bereavement of the Mother and the slayings of Leonardo and the Bridegroom, [In *Blood Wedding,* by Federico García Lorca] are we not forced to ask, "Does this mean that the primitive hunger of the blood must always be satisfied, though it destroy the man, the family, and even the society through which it flows?" But, finally, what are we moved to ask of the death of Willy Loman? To what critical human issue does it point? Or is it merely another depressing episode, and, like his life, without significance? Who is Willy Loman that attention should be paid to him?

To answer that he is three million American salesmen—at least the equal of one Theban king or one Moorish general—is to evade the question. It is also an evasion to say that Willy is a common or Lo-man and hence ineligible to be the hero of a tragedy. The tragic vision is not focussed on the station or status of man, but on the motives of his soul. The stature of Othello and Oedipus and Leonardo comes not from their place but from the intensity of their living. They have had knowledge that life is good; in them a human potential has been reached and, in the face of destruction, their manhood affirmed. It would solve our problem if we could insist that attention be paid to Willy Loman because in his living, whatever his station or work, he had lived, because in his human relations he had soared to what men are capable of. But even where he seems most successful, in the adoration given him by Biff and Happy, we know the shallowness of Willy's achievement; we know the falseness of his aspirations, and how their falsity keeps him from laying any real foundations for their future or his own.

Like Oedipus, Willy does not know who his father is or who his children are. But unlike Oedipus, who has the strength to discover the truth, as well as the strength to destroy himself, Willy has only the weakness of his ignorance. His self-destruction is not, like Othello's, an atonement and redress of balance by a figure who emerges from his torture with dearly bought wisdom; it is the despairing, ill-considered act of immaturity. If we reject Willy, it is because he is only potentially a hero. He never grows to full size, since, though he has something of the heroic spirit, he only vaguely comprehends that his life is without meaning or substance. We reject him because his life, the *unexamined* life, is not worth living. And yet, we cannot wholly reject him: the terror of Miller's vision, and the point at which it joins those of Sophocles and Shakespeare, is that it finally forces us to ask, "Have we created a society fundamentally so inimical to man that, in cutting him off from the sun and the earth, it threatens his very survival?"

Selected Criticisms

If Everyman will forgive me, in Arthur Miller's Salesman there's much of Everyman. Bothered, bewildered, but mostly bedeviled, as Willy Loman is, he's not a great deal different from the majority of his contemporaries. He, even as you and I, builds himself a shaky shelter of illusion.

You've the author's word that the motif of *Death of a Salesman* is the growth of illusion in even the most commonplace of mortals. In Willy Loman, the illusionist of the title, the individual is destroyed. And his progeny, Biff and Happy, are wrecked upon the rocks of reality.

Willy has created an image of himself which fails to correspond with Willy Loman as he is. According to the playwright, it's the size of the discrepancy that matters. In Salesman Loman, the discrepancy is so great that it finally slays him. Ironically, by his own unsteady hand.

In *Death of a Salesman*, the present and the past of Willy Loman exist concurrently—the "stream of consciousness" idea—until they collide in climax. Isn't it true that the Willy Lomans of this world are their own worst tragedy? At the Morosco, only Linda Loman can foresee the end.

And she, as wife and mother, is powerless to prevent it. This, to me, is the play's most tragic tragedy. She, too, is the play's most poignant figure. Not soon shall I forget her!

From *The New York Journal-American,* Feb. 1, 1949, p.24.

Death of a Salesman is a play written along the lines of the finest classical tragedy. It is the revelation of a man's downfall, in destruction whose roots are entirely in his own soul. The play builds to an immutable conflict where there is no resolution for this man in this life.

The play is a fervent query into the great American competitive dream of success, as it strips to the core a castaway from the race for recognition and money.

The failure of a great potential could never be so moving or so universally understandable as is the fate of Willy Loman, because his complete happiness could have been so easy to attain. He is an artisan who glories in manual effort and can be proud of the sturdy fine things he puts together out of wood and cement.

At eighteen he is introduced to the attention he might receive and the financial vistas he might travel by selling on the road. This original deception dooms him to a life of touring and a habit of prideful rationalization, until at sixty he is so far along his tangent that his efforts not to admit his resultant mediocrity are fatal.

Through most of this career runs the insistent legacy of "amounting to something" on his adopted terms, which he forces on his favorite son. With indulgent adoration he unbalances the boy, demanding a mutual idolatry which he himself inevitably fails. If young Biff steals, it is courage. If he captains a football team, the world is watching.

In the end, after repeated failure, Biff sees the truth, too late to really penetrate his father's mind. The boy's tortured efforts to explain his own little true destiny can only crack open the years-long rift, and the salesman, with all his dream's lost shadows, has no alternative to death for his peace.

Often plays have been written that crossed beyond physical actuality into the realm of memory and imagination, but it is doubtful if any has so skillfully transcended the limits of real time and space. One cannot term the chronology here a flashback technique, because the transitions are so immediate and logical.

As Willy's mind wavers under the strain of his own failure and the antagonism of his boy, he recalls the early hopeful days. The course of the play runs so smoothly that it seems one moment the two sons have gone to bed upstairs in plain sight, weary and cynical, and an instant later they are tumbling in youthful exuberance to the tune of their father's delighted flattery.

Sometimes Willy recalls the chance he once had to join his rich adventurous brother, and as his desperation increases he begs Ben for some explanation of his deep confusion.

These illuminations of the man are so exquisitely molded into the form of the play that it sweeps along like a powerful tragic symphony. The actors are attuned to the text as if they were distinct instruments. Themes rise and fade, are varied and repeated. Again as in music, an idea may be introduced as a faint echo, and afterwards developed to its fullest part in the big scheme.

From *The New York World-Telegram*, February 11, 1949, p.16.

In the end, after so much heaping of insult on injury, all one really knows about Willy Loman is that if the system doesn't kick him in the teeth he will do it himself—a well-known if wearisome tendency, that in itself might have dramatic possibilities, but that is neither particularly associated with salesmen nor adapated to the purposes of this play.

What it does lend itself to in this case is an intellectual muddle and a lack of candor that regardless of Mr. Miller's conscious intent are the main earmark of contemporary fellow-traveling. What used to be a roar has become a whine, and this particular piece of whining has been so expertly put over that it has been able to pass for something else, but behind all the fancy staging the old basic clumsiness and lack of humor are there. To be sure there are a few moments of ordinary Broadway sprightliness, as in the matter of the icebox, or Hap's little performance with the girls in the restaurant, but these are in passing.

From a review by Eleanor Clark in *Theatre Chronicle, Partisan Review,* Vol. XVI, No. 6, June 1949, pp. 631-635.

The play, it strikes us, is essentially the mother's tragedy, not Willy Loman's. Willy's plight is sad, true, but he is unimportant and too petty, commonplace, and immature to arouse more than pity, and the sons are of a piece with their father. Their aims, having been limited to their reach, stunt their stature as men and the subsequent impact of their failures on us. We can only sympathize since they reflect human frailties all too common among men. Within her circumscribed sphere of living, however, the mother makes of her love a star which her idealism places on high, and when it is destroyed her heavens are wiped out. What the mother stands for is important, and when she goes down the descent is tragic.

From a review by William Byer in *School and Society,* LXX, December 3, 1949, pp. 363-364.

Death of a Salesman is a challenge to the American dream. Lest this be misunderstood, I hasten to add that there are two versions of the American dream. The historical American dream is the promise of a land of freedom with opportunity and equality for all. This dream needs no challenge, only fulfillment. But since the Civil War, and particularly since 1900, the American dream has become distorted to the dream of business success. A distinction must be made even in this. The original premise of our dream of success—popularly represented in the original boy parables of Horatio Alger—was that enterprise, courage and hard work were the keys to success. Since the end of the First World War this too has changed. Instead of the ideals of hard work and courage, we have salesmanship. Salesmanship implies a certain element of fraud: the ability to put over or sell a commodity regardless of its intrinsic usefulness. The goal of salesmanship is to make a deal, to earn a profit—the accumulation of profit being an unquestioned end in itself.

This creates a new psychology. To place all value in the mechanical act of selling and in self-enrichment impoverishes the human beings who are rendered secondary to the deal. To possess himself fully, a man must have an intimate connection with that with which he deals as well as with the person with whom he deals. When the connection is no more than an exchange of commodities, the man himself ceases to be a man, becomes a commodity himself, a spiritual cipher.

This is a humanly untenable situation. The salesman realizes this. Since his function precludes a normal human relationship, he substitutes an imitation of himself for the real man. He sells his "personality." This "personality," now become only a means to an end—namely, the consummated sale—is a mask worn so long that it soon comes to be mistaken, even by the man who wears it, as his real face. But it is only his commercial face with a commercial smile and a commercial aura of the well-liked, smoothly adjusted, oily cog in the machine of the sales apparatus.

This leads to a behavior pattern which is ultimately doomed; not necessarily because of the economic system of which it is the human concomitant, but quite simply because a man is not a machine. The death of Arthur Miller's salesman is symbolic of the breakdown of the whole concept of salesmanship inherent in our society.

From *Lies Like Truth* by Harold Clurman
(New York: Macmillan, 1958), pp. 68-72.

Suggested Study Topics

1. Central to Willy Loman's tragedy is a fundamental confusion in the notion of what he is really selling—himself or his "line." Explain this in terms of Willy's stress on being "very well-liked" and his lack of reference to the product itself. Explain how *Death of a Salesman* may have changed your own notion of the successful salesman.

2. Linda's role is that of the profoundly compassionate and understanding wife. Do you believe her sympathies were misplaced and, in fact, reinforced Willy's illusions of himself and the world?

3. How are Happy and Biff dissimilar in their interiorization of, and eventual reaction to, their father's value system? Contrast Biff and Bernard as adolescents and adults. Is this contrast similar to, or different from, a contrast of Willy and Charley? In what way?

4. Contemporary man is said to be relegated to a secondary role compared with the machine. Miller symbolically utilizes this theme in Howard's new recorder and Willy Loman's anguish. Describe this scene, illuminating the contrasting emotions of Howard and Willy.

5. What is the significance of Willy's prodding Biff to visit Oliver? How is Miller's intention carried further by the events which follow Biff's attempt to be interviewed there? Discuss the ensuing scene, particularly highlighting Biff's struggle to grasp reality for himself and his father.

6. Willy stresses his sons' build, appearance and athletic prowess. He teaches them to wear a smile, make important contacts and, above all, to be "very well liked." Biff's stealing is part of "playing the game." In your judgment, how do these attributes compare with those praised by the general North American society? Do you feel there is a coincidence of Willy's moral values and the approved moral code of our culture?

7. In a sense, *Death of a Salesman* represents an unrelieved tragedy. Yet there is Miller's concept of salvation in the character of Biff. Describe in detail Biff's last encounter with his father, revealing Miller's interpretation of redemption.

8. To what extent does Arthur Miller hold Willy Loman responsible for his ultimate collapse against the determining power of forces beyond his control?

Bibliography

Adler, Henry. "To Hell With Society," *Tulane Drama Review* IV, 4 (May, 1960).

Bentley, Eric. *The Dramatic Event*. Boston: 1954.

Bettina, Sister M. "Willy Loman's Brother Ben: Tragic Insight in *Death of a Salesman*," *Modern Drama* IV (February, 1962).

Carson, Neil. *Arthur Miller*. New York: Grove, 1982.

Clurman, Harold. *Lies Like Truth*. New York: 1958.

Corrigan, Robert W. *Arthur Miller: A Collection of Critical Essays*. Englewood Cliffs: 1969.

Dillingham, William B. "Arthur Miller and the Loss of Consciousness," *Emory University Quarterly* XVI:40-50.

Eissenstat, Martha T. "Arthur Miller: A Bibliography," *Modern Drama* V (May, 1962).

Evans, Richard I. *Psychology and Arthur Miller*. New York: Dutton, 1969.

Ganz, Arthur. "The Silence of Arthur Miller," *Drama* Survey III (October, 1963).

Gould, Jean. *Modern American Playwrights*. New York: 1966.

Hayashi, Tetsumaro. *An Index to Arthur Miller Criticism*. New Jersey: 1976.

Hayman, Ronald. *Arthur Miller*. New York: Ungar, 1972.

Hogan, Robert. *Arthur Miller*. Minneapolis: University of Minnesota Press, 1964.

Huftel, Sheila. *Arthur Miller: The Burning Glass*. New York: 1965.

Hurrell, John D., ed. *Two Modern American Tragedies; Reviews and Criticism of "Death of a Salesman" and "A Streetcar Named Desire"*. New York: Scribner, 1961.

Martin, Robert A. *Arthur Miller: New Perspectives* Englewood Cliffs: Prentice-Hall, 1982.

McAnany, Emile G. "The Tragic Commitment: Some Notes on Arthur Miller," *Modern Drama* V (1962).

Miller, Arthur. *Arthur Miller's Collected Plays*. New York: Viking, 1977.

_____. *The Theatre Essays of Arthur Miller*. New York: Viking, 1978.

Moss, Leonard. *Arthur Miller*. New York: Twayne, 1967.

     ward. *Arthur Miller — Dramatist*. New York:
    r, 1967.

  , Benjamin. *Arthur Miller; Portrait of a Playwright*.
    New York: McKay, 1970.

Seagar, Allan. "The Creative Agony of Arthur Miller," *Esquire* LII (October, 1959).

Weales, Gerald. *American Drama Since World War II*. New York: 1962.

Welland, Dennis. *Miller: A Study of His Plays*. London: Eyre Methuen, 1979.

Wiegand, William. "Arthur Miller and the Man Who Knows," Western Review XXI (1957).